# L'CHAIM

## Margit Chinkes
## Holocaust Survival Story

by **Angelica M. Osborne**

COVER ART: Max Hugo Kühner, Margit's father, created the charcoal art featuring the Römer in the "old city" of Frankfurt, Germany in 1979. Hugo lived in Frankfurt from 1930 until his death in 1990. He became a prominent citizen of Frankfurt, owning two well-known restaurants—one of which became a subject of a German television series.

ISBN: 978-1-59152-199-0

Published by Angelica M. Osborne

For more information or to order extra copies of this book call Farcountry Press toll free at (800) 821-3874.

s**w**eetgrassbooks
an imprint of Farcountry Press
Produced by Sweetgrass Books.
PO Box 5630, Helena, MT 59604; (800) 821-3874; www.sweetgrassbooks.com.

The views expressed by the author/publisher in this book do not necessarily represent the views of, nor should be attributed to, Sweetgrass Books. Sweetgrass Books is not responsible for the content of the author/publisher's work.

Produced and printed in the United States of America.

21  20  19  18  17      1  2  3  4  5

# Prologue

A fourteen-year-old girl is walking hurriedly home from school in late July 1944 in Frankfurt am Main, Germany. Her name is Margit, and all she knows is that World War II is raging across Europe; Germany is being bombed and invaded by Allied and Russian troops. She must get home to help her grandma, her Oma. But as Margit walks, she is stopped and arrested by the German Gestapo and they force her to go with them to a juvenile detention center. She doesn't understand why she is being detained; she is certain that she has not done anything wrong.

Margit Chinkes, later to become Margit Pascetti, is my mother.

Many great books have been written about the Holocaust and Holocaust survivors. My mother's story was buried in her mind and largely remained there. She could not talk about her past and the pain she suffered. For her, it was better to "go on with life." She said that you couldn't change a situation but had to make the best of it.

Because I was my mother's eldest daughter, my children coaxed me to write her story for my grandchildren. It is a unique family story that needs to be told and not forgotten. I also want to give my grandchildren—Margit's great-grandchildren—a written story for them to hold onto. They, too, might be faced with obstacles in their lives. I hope my mother's story will give them courage and persistence to hold onto faith and do what they must do to be successful in their lives.

My research revealed the incredible spirit behind my mother's amazing life. She never had any self-pity but had a huge reservoir of resilience, laughter, and courage that enabled her to manage many difficult circumstances.

During my research I felt like I was in an "Amazing Race," running from one clue to the next. My husband Tom has been in this race with me all the way. This book is a factual account of Margit's life, particularly the previously undocumented period of her Nazi incarceration, written with love and in honor of her inspiring spirit.

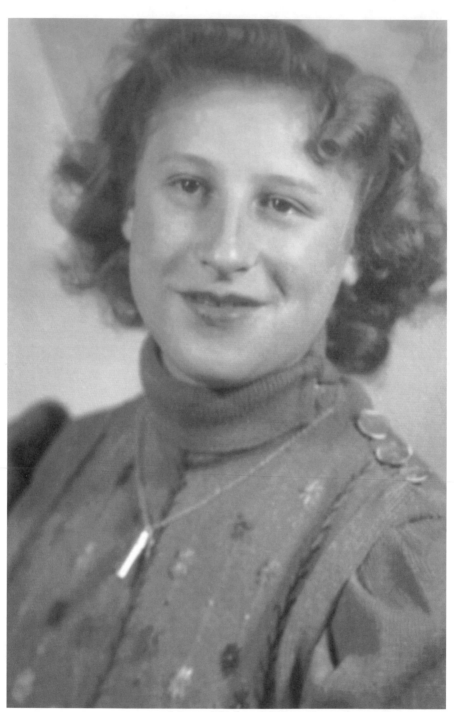

*Margit Chinkes, 1946*

# CHAPTER ONE

# Introduction of Margit Chinkes Pascetti

≈⟨◊⟩≈

I discovered the details of my mother Margit's story many years after she died. The more I learned the more amazed I became that she survived, let alone led what appeared to me to be a very normal life. My research revealed not only how many and how severe the challenges were that she encountered but that she met them with great resilience, courage, and perseverance, attempting to always do what she thought was right. Margit had the determination and strength to make the best out of difficult situations.

My mom didn't want to talk about her past. Many people with deeply troubling experiences choose to forget in order to free their minds and live in the present. I only knew a few fragments of her early life story. In writing Margit's story, I probably learned more of the details about her life and survival than she herself could have told me. It was an amazing journey of discovery for me. I've become my mom's memory bank, and I have shed many tears over the terrors and triumphs revealed in this process.

I didn't fully know what I was undertaking, but I decided that her life story should not be forgotten. My decision to write this book germinated from the urging of my adult children, and was propelled into action by a conviction received during a spiritual retreat. That part of the story, my own, is told in the Epilogue.

To my young grandchildren, your heritage is important to know because it is a special bond that connects you to me, to my mother, and to all of your ancestors. None of you have grown up in a Jewish household. Through my mother and me, you carry Jewish ancestry and Jewish genetics. Like me, you may be surprised at this and wonder what it means. You would not be who you are if your great-grandmother did not survive her childhood. This story will show you that the part of her that is in you is a powerful source of strength. This story is part of your heritage.

Before telling Margit's life story, I want the reader to get to know her better by sharing my stories and impressions of her.

Family was extremely important to Margit. After World War II the only immediate family she had in Germany was her father, Max Hugo Kühner (referred to as Hugo), and her grandmother, Sophie Bottner, whom she called Oma. She loved her Oma, the woman who raised her, and I don't feel that Margit would have left Germany while she was alive. Her beloved Oma died in 1948 after breaking a hip. Just one year later, Margit left Germany to live in the United States.

I don't really know how close Margit felt to her father. He treated her well, but he never spent much time with her and avoided a big role in her upbringing. Most perplexing to me is how Margit could have been taken by the Gestapo while her father was serving in the German military. I always wondered if he did anything to prevent this. But, to all appearances, this did not bother Margit.

My sense is that she put her father, Hugo, on a pedestal after being away from him for years. She did not acknowledge the difficult things about him from the wartime and buried them—something my siblings and I could not understand. But, as I believe her story will bear out, she did not hold onto hurts or dwell on past injustices.

Our nuclear family was always her first priority, but she also reached out to any of her or my dad, Angelo Pascetti's, extended family that she could find. After the war she immigrated with me, a baby, to the United States. Once here, my dad's family welcomed her to their home so she could adapt and get acquainted with the different lifestyle. They were her only family living in America.

As a girl, I remember that Margit wrote letters every week to family in Europe—my dad's family, her father, and her half-sister. In spite of my father's reticence about traveling to Europe, she found my dad's family in a small village near the Adriatic Sea in Italy sometime in the late 1980s. Margit, my father, and his sister, Carmen, made a "cold call" visit to them. In spite of the language barrier, all doubts were dispelled that we were really family when my dad and Nicola, his cousin, stood side by side.

Margit wrote often to her long-distance friends; she wanted to maintain her connections. I can imagine the fun she would have had with email.

Margit loved animals. I don't ever remember being without a dog when I was growing up. She had a soft heart when it came to any animal. One day we were eating dinner with the radio playing in the background. The announcer was describing a German shepherd puppy that was abandoned. Margit jumped up from the table and went to the animal shelter where the dog was located and brought it home. I grew up with that German shepherd puppy, which we called Dash.

After we all grew up and left home, Mom found a poodle at the shelter and brought the little dog home. But afterwards, the original owners found out about the dog being adopted and decided they wanted the dog back. After they retrieved the dog, Mom somehow heard that it was being abused. She found out where the dog was living and went there. She found the dog chained to a chair and the children were kicking it. I don't know how, but somehow that dog came home with my mother! She named her Shu Shu and loved that dog until the day it died.

We grew up with birds and fish, and we raised rabbits. I also remember having a goat. When he died by falling off his box, my dad told me he became the cloud in the sky I was looking at.

Margit was a good cook and loved food. She learned to cook in America by watching other people cook and by tasting the food. Her attitude, though, toward food was the more the better.

She had a green thumb, and her gardening skill produced flowers and vegetables even in Leadville, Colorado's altitude of 10,150 feet, an elevation that presents a challenge to any gardener. Margit spent hours outside working in the garden or flowerbeds wearing her big sun hat. All the neighbors loved her red lettuce from the garden. She loved fresh vegetables and fruit and preserved many jars of both over the years. Our family went to Grand Junction, Colorado, to pick peaches, and then we canned them. We drove south into the hills around Buena Vista to pick piñon nuts. Margit enjoyed fishing, just for the joy of eating fresh trout. She froze them in milk cartons, which she presented to visiting relatives as a gift. Margit was a gatherer.

My mom and dad made "home brew" before microbrewing was popular. The house smelled like a brewery, which was an embarrassment to me when my friends came for a visit. The house not only smelled like a brewery during the fermentation process, but inevitably a beer bottle would explode in the living room closet because it got too hot. They also made root beer. To this day, I love homemade root beer.

Her letters to me early in my marriage were filled with the week's menu for her and my dad. As she aged, she became more fixated on food. When she died, my siblings and I helped my dad clean out the house. We found three freezers filled to the top with food. Cupboards in the basement were stacked full of food; they couldn't hold any more. Some of the canned goods were so old that they exploded in the storage space, which created quite a mess.

During the holidays, Margit spent days preparing food. She invited all of her friends over for German music, visiting, and lots of food. The entire table was filled with turkey, ham, salads, potivca, and German cakes and candies. She made Challah, a Jewish holiday bread. Her recipe is titled *Oma's Challah bread*. I do not know where she got that recipe; it's doubtful her Oma made Challah as she was not Jewish. On Christmas Eve all the candles in the house were lit with German and Italian Christmas carols playing on the phonograph. Margit had many German friends who always came to our home for the festive activities. Her German American friend Crystal said Margit was the best friend a person could have.

Margit had many friends, young and old. She helped one German friend get her American citizenship. All her friendships were lasting relationships. Today, I continue to keep in contact with several of Margit's friends. It would make her happy to know I still write Christmas cards to some of her friends and that I call her very best friend from Germany at various times.

Margit loved the Germany she left. She was so proud to be German. Margit loved her German music, and during any car trip, a German tape would be playing! She never lost her German accent, and to this day, every time I hear someone speak with a German accent I think of her. Margit thought that German products were always the best. If she could choose to buy something American or German, her country of origin would win.

Margit was a content person. She didn't complain about her life even when it was hard, like when my dad was participating in a mining strike for six months and had no work. Margit was a hard worker. She woke up every morning before my dad left for work (5:30 A.M.) and made his breakfast and his lunch. She never went back to bed, as she had work she needed to do.

When I was growing up, a wife and husband had distinct roles in the home, more than is the case today. My mother took care of my dad. It was a standing joke between them that she did everything for him but chew his food! At night my dad sat in his recliner and mom brought him the biggest bowl of ice cream. No one ever got more than my dad. But at the same time, when it came to remodeling our house, my mom was right beside my dad helping him. He would do the heavy work, but she always gave him a hand.

I only knew a small part of my mom's life—basically, the part a child knows growing up in the family. I knew she had suffered during World War II and lived in two concentration camps when she was fourteen years old. But it was not something she wanted to talk about. I only got the smallest glimpses from her. Like other people who survived difficult ordeals in their lives, I think my mom understood that she could not change the past; therefore, it was of no use for her to dwell on what had occurred. She chose to live in the present and plan for a good future for her family.

In November 1995, when she was dying of malignant melanoma while living in my home, she finally said she would record her story for me. She attempted this task, but her voice was so weak that we could not hear what she said. What was in the deep shadows of Margit's memories? After her death I still wondered about her story.

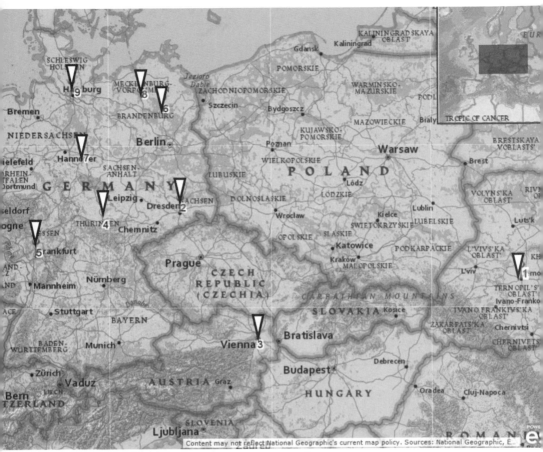

*Map Locations of Events*

LEGEND

1. Tarnopol, Ukraine
2. Dresden, Germany
3. Vienna, Austria
4. Bad Tennstedt, Germany
5. Frankfurt, Germany
6. Ravensbrück Camp, Germany
7. Salzgitter-Watenstedt Camp, Germany
8. Malchow, Germany
9. Neuengamme Camp, Germany

# CHAPTER TWO

# Frieda Chinkes and
# Max Hugo Kühner

❧

I will now tell you Margit's story as I know it. I've done much research to find as many facts about her early life as possible. I am astonished and overwhelmed by my mother's will to survive the tragedies that beset her early life.

Margit's mother was Frieda Chinkes. Frieda was born on February 27, 1910, in Tarnopol, Poland, to her parents, Izaak Chinkes and Marjem (Kuj) Chinkes (Matrikelamt Der Israelitischen Kultusgemeinde in Wien). Marjem and Izaak were married January 24, 1909, in Tarnopol with the marriage certificate signed by Rabbi Babad Szymon (Republic of Poland). (Margit's family tree follows.) Copies of the references herein are included in Appendix A.

The archives of the City of Vienna show that Frieda had two siblings: Max born in 1912 in Tarnopol, and Anna born in 1917 (Chancellor, Magistratsasbteilung 8). Frieda's parents immigrated to Vienna from Tarnopol in March 1913. Marjem became a widow in 1919. She remarried Izaak Flanzgraben on November 3, 1920; they lived in the Jewish quarter in Vienna.

Margit's father was Max Hugo Kühner, born on June 28, 1907, in Dresden, Germany, to Sophie Agnes Kühner (Kühner). Sophie was divorced from her husband, Friedrich Bottner, at the time of the birth of Hugo. Hugo was the youngest of three other siblings, two brothers and one sister. All were much older, with his sister, the closest in age, fifteen years older than Hugo.

In his unpublished memoir (Kühner, translated by Werner Will), Hugo wrote that he had been traveling to Africa and India for adventure and contracted malaria. He was returning to his home in Germany to recuperate, but upon arrival in Vienna he became too weak to journey any farther. He rented a furnished room in the main quarter of the Jewish population. His room was in the same apartment building in which Frieda and her family lived. Hugo wrote that Frieda nursed him back to health. He was evidently a very charming and captivating young man. Affection grew between them and they became intimate. But not long after, Hugo left Vienna, continuing his journey to Hungary.

In his memoir Hugo wrote that he received a letter from Vienna informing him that Frieda had become pregnant. The letter stated that Frieda's parents

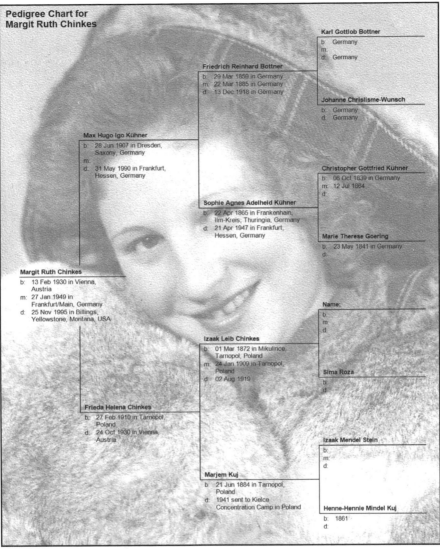

**Pedigree Chart for Margit Ruth Chinkes**

**Margit Ruth Chinkes**
b: 13 Feb 1930 in Vienna, Austria
m: 27 Jan 1949 in Frankfurt/Main, Germany
d: 25 Nov 1995 in Billings, Yellowstone, Montana, USA

**Max Hugo Igo Kühner**
b: 28 Jun 1907 in Dresden, Saxony, Germany
m:
d: 31 May 1990 in Frankfurt, Hessen, Germany

**Friedrich Reinhard Bottner**
b: 29 Mar 1859 in Germany
m: 22 Mar 1885 in Germany
d: 13 Dec 1918 in Germany

**Karl Gottlob Bottner**
b: Germany
m:
d: Germany

**Johanne Chrislisme-Wunsch**
b: Germany
d: Germany

**Sophie Agnes Adelheid Kühner**
b: 22 Apr 1865 in Frankenhain, Ilm-Kreis, Thuringia, Germany
d: 21 Apr 1947 in Frankfurt, Hessen, Germany

**Christopher Gottfried Kühner**
b: 06 Oct 1839 in Germany
m: 12 Jul 1884
d:

**Marie Therese Goering**
b: 23 May 1841 in Germany
d:

**Frieda Helena Chinkes**
b: 27 Feb 1910 in Tarnopol, Poland
d: 24 Oct 1930 in Vienna, Austria

**Izaak Leib Chinkes**
b: 01 Mar 1872 in Mikulince, Tarnopol, Poland
m: 24 Jan 1909 in Tarnopol, Poland
d: 02 Aug 1919

**Name:**
b:
m:
d:

**Sima Roza**
b:
d:

**Marjem Kuj**
b: 21 Jun 1884 in Tarnopol, Poland
d: 1941 sent to Kielce Concentration Camp in Poland

**Izaak Mendel Stein**
b:
m:
d:

**Henne-Hennie Mindel Kuj**
b: 1861
d:

*Family tree of Margit Chinkes*

disowned her because of her affair with a "goy." Even worse, he was informed Frieda wanted to commit suicide. Hugo reported that he immediately returned to Vienna to marry her. He met a rabbi who advised him how to reestablish normal relations between Frieda and her parents. But, he said that her parents were "very pious" and did not listen to the rabbi's advice.

Although a German Evangelical Lutheran by his upbringing, Hugo then got the idea that he would convert to Judaism. Over some weeks, he undertook a study of Jewish rituals and customs. He submitted to circumcision. One day he reached his goal—standing in front of the Torah in the largest synagogue in Vienna where he accepted the Jewish faith.

His memoir states that he and Frieda were joined in a ritual marriage of Jewish faith in the apartment of her parents. But the marriage was not recognized by the State of Austria or by the Jewish community. There is no record of a marriage between Hugo and Frieda in the Vienna city archives or in the Vienna Jewish archives. In the early 1930s social norms were not accepting of interfaith marriages, especially between Jews and German Christians. Hugo realized, it seems, that just because he learned something of the rituals of the Jewish faith, it did not make him Jewish. As a practical matter, Hugo needed to apply for residency, and with the help of his new in-laws he was able to get a job in a paper production plant.

Margit Chinkes was born on February 13, 1930. Frieda was a twenty-year-old seamstress at the time of her daughter's birth. The Vienna Jewish records indicate that Hugo was not present when she gave birth to Margit. Hugo is also not listed on Margit's birth certificate. Frieda had a Jewish naming ceremony for the baby, which gave her the name Anni Ruth Chinkes. The name Anni was given to her in honor of Frieda's sister who died in 1927 when she was ten years old. However, Margit was the name given on her birth certificate. I do not believe my mother was aware of the naming ceremony, which gave her a Hebrew name. Hugo only called her Margit. He never gave her the Kühner surname. All documents for Margit have her last name as Chinkes.

Frieda continued living in the Jewish section of Vienna in an apartment mostly by herself and occasionally with Hugo. The apartment is still in the Jewish section of town today. The tall apartment buildings looked like they were elegant and well-kept at one time. On a 2014 trip, Tom and I were able to go into the apartment building when a gentleman saw us taking pictures of it from the outside. He invited us into the inside court. I was amazed to see a black spiral staircase; the building had traces of bygone beauty. It must have been beautiful once, but when we visited, it was in need of repair and renovation.

Hugo was ambitious and enjoyed the freedom of a single man though he had married Frieda. He went his own way, forcing Frieda to learn to cope with the demands of a new infant and to provide an income for herself and the baby. This statement is based both on my research as well as my personal knowledge of Hugo. He did not want to be attached to a woman and a baby. The Vienna archives records indicate that Frieda and Hugo lived together from February 1929 through April 1929 and again from October 1929 to January 1930. They were also living together June 1930 through October 1930 when she followed through on her earlier threat and committed suicide.

The City of Vienna archives reports that Frieda's death occurred on October 24, 1930. The archives contain the following undated excerpt from a Vienna newspaper of that time, absent the initial portion of the article:

*...week did not bring the promised contribution for the child; there was yesterday evening a loud argument between the two (Frieda and Hugo), which continued on the street. At seven o'clock in the evening, the couple was observed arguing vehemently at the Augarten Bridge. Finally, the woman tore herself loose, ran away and threw herself into the Danube canal.*

*The woman left a fare well letter, addressed to the afore-mentioned woman with whom she was presently residing, with the following content. Dear Mrs. B., if you are really willing to accept my child, would you please take it completely and don't let Mr. K. have it, because he will destroy the child. Have him arrested. He has two young lives on his conscience. Everything that one will find with him belongs to me. Keep it for the child later on.* Source: Article from the Archives of the City of Vienna and State Archives under the heading of "Historical Viennese Registration Material (translation by Werner Will) (Chancellor, Magistratsasbteilung 8)

I was totally blown away when I read this account from the Vienna archives! It left me with so many questions: Who was Mrs. B? And who were the two lives on Hugo's hands?

My grandfather, the only person I knew with a direct connection to the actual events, has in his memoir a wildly different and almost bizarre account of Frieda's suicide. He states,

*One day when I arrived home after work, I entered the apartment and found the child in the crib. The meal was on the table with a newspaper. Everything was as it should be, except my wife was missing. I waited for hours, but all my inquiries were negative. Then the police came and reported that my wife had fallen off a steep cliff along the Danube, where we had often walked. As my wife could not swim, it was surprising that she drifted several hundred meters downstream, and tried to hold onto a scaffold that was used to do some bridge repair work. Several men heard a cry for help and tried to climb down into the water. But before they reached her, my wife must have lost her strength and drowned. Weeks later I recognized the dress which was shown to me (it was a colorful silk dress), and I discovered that my wife had been found and had been buried. I put in a request to exhume the body and bury her in a Jewish cemetery. This request was granted and executed.*

Adding to the mystery surrounding Frieda's demise, her death certificate is dated June 11, 1931, about seven months after the date of death reported by the archives. The certificate notes that it was a delayed death certificate for unknown reasons. The newspaper reported that Frieda's death occurred on

*Apartment building of Frieda and Hugo, 1930*
*Franz Hochedlinger 3, Vienna, Austria*

October 24, 1930. Perhaps a delayed death certificate was issued when her body was recovered from the river and identified.

My mind and my heart have struggled with Frieda's suicide, between the "shattered love" account of the newspaper and Hugo's "tragic surprise" version. My own work as a maternal/child health nurse tells me Frieda probably succumbed to post-partum depression in the grayness of the Vienna winter. She may have been sleep deprived and stressed with the realization she would have to raise Margit alone. She likely saw no way to reconcile her Jewish life with her new life as a single mother, facing disapproval and rejection in every quarter.

From the newspaper account, I believe Frieda knew of another child fathered by Hugo and that he walked out on that mother and left her without any support. She could only anticipate with Hugo's history that she too would ultimately be responsible for the upbringing of Margit. Frieda evidently planned her suicide; she had written a note prior to her and Hugo going to the Augarten Bridge from which she jumped into the sluggish and green Danube Canal.

My sadness over my grandmother's abbreviated life was deepened when, during our 2014 visit to Vienna, we sought out and found Frieda's final resting place. The Jewish cemetery is a separate extension of the Catholic cemetery on the southern outskirts of the city. It took a couple of bus changes to get there. Tom and I used the paperwork identifying the location of her plot, but, of course, it was confusing to find while wandering on the grounds. With the help of the cemetery caretakers, we were led to an old, overgrown section. After carefully counting plot numbers, the caretakers pointed to an empty spot of tall grass.

Other graves nearby had markers from the early 1930s, suggesting we were in the right area. But no marker stood on Frieda's plot. We stood there in the late afternoon, sad to think that maybe no one cared enough to leave some memorial of her. But we were also overawed by the sensation that finally, my life and hers intersected, at least in this tiny space. We said a prayer and I piled some stones on her grave, in the Jewish tradition. But I told myself and Tom that we would do the right thing by her memory and eventually get a marker on her grave.

It was very troubling and humbling to admit that the heartbreaking closure to my grandmother's suffering on this earth was just the beginning of my mother's. I would like to know if Frieda thought that her baby would be in better hands after she was gone. Her suicide note clearly indicated she had grave concerns over who got custody of her baby.

Margit's custody hung in a very delicate balance among the parties of Hugo, Frieda's family, the State of Austria, and some unknown Mrs. B. Unraveling this fateful custody muddle involves two separate subplots, first, the story of who is the "second young life" on Hugo's hands, and second, the fractious historical accounts surrounding the custody of Margit following Frieda's suicide.

## Margit's Half-Sister

I feel that Frieda knew about Hugo's past and that the two young lives she referred to were Margit and another child fathered by Hugo.

About four years before Hugo met Frieda, he met Clara Brehme, and in 1926 Hugo had a daughter with Clara (Grosch). The daughter's name was Ruth. Similar to Hugo's behavior with Frieda and Margit, Hugo left Clara and abandoned Ruth. Ruth's grandmother, Mrs. Berta Brehme, took over the parenting duties. I can't help but wonder if Frieda knew of Ruth being raised by her grandmother, Mrs. Brehme, and wanted the two half-sisters to be raised together. She may have been the Mrs. B. that Frieda referred to in her suicide note.

Years later, Ruth's son, Wolfgang, wrote to me, "Her Oma raised Ruth, as her own mother could not raise her, as she was a single mother." Hugo had left Ruth's pregnant mother also without any financial support or any other support. Ruth's Oma was a midwife who was married to Wilhelm Brehme, a shoemaker. They made their home in Bad Tennstedt, a small town thirty-two minutes from Erfurt, Germany.

Margit did not become aware of Ruth until the early 1950s (more on that later); however, it appears that the two sisters met long before that. Ruth told me that she recalled a playdate when she was seven years old with a then two-year-old Margit in Erfurt. Margit was too young to remember, but Ruth recalled pushing Margit in a stroller. At the time the two sisters only lived thirty minutes from each other. So it seems that Mrs. Brehme was aware of Margit, and so it is possible that Frieda was aware of Mrs. Brehme and Ruth as well.

## Hugo Obtained and Dodged Custody

Frieda's last wishes were not fulfilled. After Frieda's death Hugo was given custody of Margit. However, he still did not want to care for her. He wrote in his memoir that he was desperate finding himself alone in a big city with a child. Dodging his responsibilities once again, Hugo sought out his childless sister, Hedwig, who lived in Erfurt, Germany. Erfurt is the capital city of the German Thuringia region. It is the place where Martin Luther studied and became a monk, planting the roots of the Protestant Reformation movement.

Hedwig always wanted a child, so she agreed to care for Margit. Her ex-husband had children, but she had none of her own. She was divorced and now had time to love and care for a child.

I found court documents that gave Hedwig custody of Margit dated April 20, 1931 (Chancellor, Magistratsasbteilung 8). Margit lived with Hedwig and

Hugo's mother, Sophie Agnes Bottner. Together they were living in Erfurt, Germany. Margit was fifteen months old when Hedwig was granted the guardianship. Hugo did not live with Hedwig and his mother in Erfurt; he continued his life as a single man living in Frankfurt, Germany, running a trucking business. Sadly, to my knowledge, he did not participate in the care of his daughter at this time.

## Margit's Memory of Her Custody Story

Margit knew her mother's name and also knew that her mother committed suicide by drowning in the Danube Canal when she was a mere eight months old. She was a child when her father told her about her birth mother; she had no memory of her mother except for what Hugo had told her. He related to Margit that her mother was an Orthodox Jew but was disowned by her parents when she became involved with him and then had his baby. Margit also understood from Hugo that Frieda's parents did not want to raise her. When I finally met members of Frieda's family in April 2016, their recollection was that it was Hugo who didn't allow the maternal grandparents to raise Margit. Chapter 11 gives the complete story of my discovery of Frieda's family.

## Continuing the Story of Margit's Early Years

Hugo's perfect solution to Margit's care was not destined to last. In 1937 Hedwig died suddenly of an illness. Margit was seven years of age. When I was growing up, my mom spoke fondly of her Aunt Hedwig and knew she was not her mother.

Following Hedwig's death, Hugo had no choice but to have his mother and Margit move in with him in Frankfurt. Sophie, Hugo's mother, was probably around seventy-three years old when she had sole care of Margit. It must not have been easy for her, as Hugo was not home much of the time. When he was home, he did not participate in Margit's care but showered his daughter with gifts and pets.

Despite her father's frequent absences, Margit had a good life living with her Oma and her father. She never had to learn to cook, as her Oma did it all. Hugo hired help for household duties for his mother, as he knew she couldn't do everything. Margit attended school at Liebfrauen Schule as a Christian-Protestant girl. She had no association with the Jewish religion or Jewish tradition. It was doubtful that she had Jewish friends at that time.

In 1939 Hugo got married legally for the first time. He does not mention his wife's name in his memoir, but he does say that he now had help with his mother and daughter, who then was nine years of age. This probably was a marriage of convenience. Based on a letter from Margit to Sophie (Chapter 3), I believe Hugo's wife's name was Hanni.

In 1941 Hugo was called to serve in the German military. Since 1939 Germany had been at war in Europe, and in 1941 Germany declared war on the United States of America. During World War II all major European countries were at war with Germany and Italy.

Adolf Hitler was the dictator of Germany; his war machine was in full force. He had perverted radical ideas of German Nationalism and anti-Semitism. He believed Germans were "racially superior" and Jews were "inferior." It was against the law to be Jewish (Museum, Washington D.C. Holocaust). Hitler not only targeted the Jewish people, but people with disabilities and gypsies and some of the Slavic people. The Nazi party established concentration camps to detain opponents whose political and religious beliefs were not tolerated by the Nazi party.

Jewish people were rounded up, forced from their homes into ghettos isolated from their original neighborhoods or cities. All people were forced to register with the German police. They were given cards with their photographs and their identified nationality; the cards were stamped with an official stamp corresponding to the police station where they were issued. When confronted by officials people needed to produce their cards.

Jewish people were forced to wear a yellow armband with black outlines. "Jude" was written in the center of the Star of David. This was one of the tactics of the Nazi party to isolate Jews from the rest of the population. It enabled the Nazi government to identify, concentrate, and ultimately murder the Jews of Europe.

Jewish people were threatened with severe punishment, which included death by shooting if they did not wear the badge. Separating the Jewish population from the other residents of the particular country was just the beginning of what was called the "Final Solution" for Jewish people (Museum, Washington D.C. Holocaust). By the end of the war, the Nazis had killed approximately five to six million Jews, which was two-thirds of the Jewish population in Europe. An estimated five million additional people were killed in the Holocaust in addition to the groups mentioned above; these victims included Jehovah Witnesses, homosexuals, disabled people, and gypsies.

Non-Jewish people became fearful of associating with Jewish people because if they were thought to be sympathizers, they too would be targets of the Nazi police for punishment.

Fourteen-year-old Margit lived in a German household. Her father served in the Germany military. Margit had been raised as a Christian-Protestant. She had no awareness of the Jewish religion and no association with any Jewish people. Margit was not wearing a yellow armband with the black star when the Gestapo picked her up.

# CHAPTER THREE

# Detention

ꙮ

Hugo stated in his memoir that his new wife became dissatisfied with the living arrangement with his mother Sophie and that she had to care for Margit while Hugo was away fulfilling his military obligations. She wanted to move Sophie to a retirement home and have the apartment to herself. The wife spoke to the landlady and tried to get Sophie evicted from the apartment. Hugo became aware of the situation and presented documents to the landlady showing that he was the sole owner of the apartment, which allowed his mother to remain there. This infuriated the wife! Furthermore, Hugo let his wife know that he planned to divorce her. Hugo said in his memoir that his wife hated him for not putting his mother in a retirement home.

Margit and her friend Margot Turner recalled that Hugo's wife wanted revenge against Hugo. Margot and Margit became best friends when Margit moved to Frankfurt and remained friends until Margit's death. They were similar in age and played often together.

The story of Margit's betrayal came to me from several sources, including the accounts of Hugo, Margot, and Margit's letter sent later sent from the detention center (Turner). Hugo's wife told a gossipy neighbor that Hugo's child Margit was half Jewish. The wife knew the neighbor would report Margit to the officials. Frieda's Jewish blood made Margit a person of mixed race, and therefore one of those to be exterminated by the German Nationalist government. Reporting such "undesirables" to the Nazi authorities elevated this woman's status in the eyes of the government.

So this is how Margit came to be picked up by the SS and sent to live in the juvenile detention center at fourteen years old. She had no one to rescue her or any power or control to change the situation. From her correspondence, of which I have copies, it appears that she tried to make the best of it, and she realized that tears weren't going to solve her problem.

Margit was able to contact Sophie, her Oma, by writing a letter one week after the detention (Appendix A).

August 1, 1944

*Dear Oma,*
*I just realized everything is over for me. I have to go to camp for a few years.*
*The social worker for Juveniles was here to talk to me. If Hanni would*
*have been here, I would have had it out with her as it's because of her I'm*
*in this situation. I can hardly keep from crying, but the tears won't solve*
*my problems! My case is with the secret state police or secret service on*
*Linden street. Please go back to this place and to get there take streetcar #3.*
*I beg you to do me one more favor and go there! I personally can't do any-*
*thing as it out of my hands. Greetings to you and all of my friends. Margit*

One week later Margit wrote a second letter to her father (Appendix A).

August 8, 1944

*Dear Papa,*
*Last Sunday Oma came to visit. I was pleased about it. I could talk, but*
*not the way I wanted as we were never alone and to top it off she is hard*
*of hearing. I assume you've received my last letter. In the mean time I have*
*no choice but to be strong, hold on and accept the situation. When I hear*
*about the things these other girls have done to be here, I feel like I'm in the*
*wrong place! I wish I had some kind of a solution about this whole situa-*
*tion. Today the weather is delightful, but we are only allowed to walk to*
*the balcony. I will end this letter. Greetings from Margit.*

As she wrote in her letter to her Oma, she knew she was going to a camp.
What is the camp? What happens at the camp? Where is the camp? No one
outside the camps talked about the camps except perhaps in whispers. German
citizens were very much afraid to acknowledge there were sinister things going
on at the camps. They knew if they spoke out against the camps that they, too,
could go.

Margit was transported by train from Frankfurt via Leipzig to Ravensbrück
Concentration Camp after she wrote her letter to her father on August 8, 1944. I
found her name on the transport ledger in Ravensbrück. These records, attached
in Appendix A, show that she was part of a 100-prisoner transport. She arrived
there October 15, 1944.

Margit's whereabouts cannot be determined for a period of two months
and seven days, between the detention center in Frankfurt and her arrival at
the Ravensbrück Concentration Camp. Margot told me that she tried to
go visit Margit in the detention center in early August 1944, but Margit was
already gone.

The deportations to the camps were referred to as "evacuations" or "resettlements." The prisoner transport trains in 1942-1945 consisted of freight cars. The civil servants of the German train system ensured the running of the trains (Steinke). They evidently needed to have 100 people per wagon or car in order to be paid. So the train stopped at various places to pick up people for deportation to have the correct number.

It appears that sometime between the middle of August and mid-October Margit was forced to board a train without knowing where it was headed. The trip to Ravensbrück was approximately 630 kilometers (391 miles). People were not given any food or water and were crowded into the trains. They probably tolerated a great stench from urine and excrement as the people were only provided a bucket as a sanitary concession. The freight train moved slowly, starting and stopping frequently to allow German soldiers to board the train. Doors and windows remained locked. People were not allowed to leave the train.

Margit was fourteen years old and alone on the transport train. She didn't have a mother to console her, a father to look to for support, or a sister or brother to hang on to. She was crammed into the train with not even a friend to talk to. She didn't even know where she was going. Margit's fear of the unknown must have greatly deepened during her separation from her family and the more than two-month transport.

The transport made an indelible imprint on Margit's memory, one of only a handful of stories she told us as children: on the train trip she had her fortune read by a gypsy. The gypsy told her she wouldn't die in the camp. She was also told that when it was time to get in the lines for where they were going, to get in the line of Polish women. I imagine that a child from a German Protestant background of those days would have been astounded to meet a fortune teller, and even more astounded to have her future foretold to her.

Margit did get a letter out from the train to her close friend, Margot Turner (Turner). Margit wrote that she was on a train with lots of people crammed in. She didn't know where she was going. This letter came to Margot without a stamp. People got letters out of the train by handing them to people out the windows—trusting to the strangers' goodwill. Margot told me that she gave this letter to Hugo, but it did not survive the years.

What happened to Margit once she arrived at the Ravensbrück camp, I could only surmise based on the descriptions given at the Ravensbrück Memorial, as she never spoke about the situation.

From the Memorial accounts and from books I've read, this is what the prisoners were made to endure. They were first ordered to stand in lines, and an SS guard pointed to which direction each person must go. Children, the elderly, and the disabled were pointed one direction, to the gas chambers. Children under the age of thirteen were considered "useless eaters"—1.5 million children were killed during the Holocaust. Germany needed a labor force for the war; non-Jewish adolescent thirteen to eighteen years old were used for forced labor (Museum, Washington D.C. Holocaust). Margit at fourteen years old must have looked strong. The prisoners were registered in a utility building and stripped of any belongings; their heads were shaved and they were forced to take cold showers. After the shower, women had to remain naked while they underwent a medical examination. They were given prisoner uniforms and assigned to one of the huts for new arrivals (Eschebach).

People were each given a number, and in some camps this number was tattooed on the person. A prisoner was only known as a number, which was a way to dehumanize them. Margit did not have a tattoo. I do not know why, other than tattoos weren't done in all the concentration camps. Auschwitz was one of the concentration camps that tattooed numbers on the prisoners.

Margit's number in Ravensbrück was 079046. She was not called by her name, only by number. Records at Ravensbrück show that she was first labeled as a political prisoner. There was correspondence indicating the authorities were trying to ascertain her correct classification, which was later changed to "mixed race." She was given a different number when she was transferred to Watenstedt/Salzgitter: 009598. She was in block 9 in Salzgitter. The prisoner number signifies the number of people in that particular camp at the time of her admission.

I believe that Margit's head was shaved based on an experience in our house when I was a young girl. One time my dad was giving my brother Gerald a haircut. Gerald wiggled around and my dad nicked his head, giving him a bald spot. Dad got angry and decided to shave all his hair off. My mom burst into tears when she saw her bald son; it must have brought back many unpleasant memories to her. I never saw my mom cry about anything, so I was really horrified. I didn't understand at the time why seeing my brother's bald head would make her cry. I was told by her friend Margot that Margit was very proud of her hair when it grew back after being in the concentration camp.

Heinrich Himmler, a high-ranking Nazi commander who was one of Hilter's most evil and feared supporters of the Reich, ordered gas chambers to be built at Ravensbrück in November 1944 for efficiency of extermination (Saidel). According to a survivor, Gemma LaGuardia Gluck, the gas room resembled a bathroom and its door was labeled "bathroom." The victims were told to undress, given a piece of soap and a towel, and were led to the "showers." Instead of water, the gas was turned on. During Easter week in 1945 the crematory burned day and night. As the Allied and Russian armies closed in, the Nazis wanted to get rid of as much "evidence" as they could (Saidel).

Margit's transfers in and out of Ravensbrück seem now to have been miraculously timed. She arrived in October 1944 and was transferred to Watenstedt/Salzgitter in November 1944, just as the gas chamber was being constructed in Ravensbrück. In the shuffling of prisoners near the close of the war, she was returned to Ravensbrück in April 1945. But, just prior to the Russians' arrival in April, the gas chamber itself was totally destroyed by Nazi commanders to obliterate evidence. Margit escaped the awful fate of the gas chamber.

*Ravensbrück Memorial*

# CHAPTER FOUR

# The Camps

M̲argit was in Ravensbrück for approximately one month. She was transferred to a sub-camp of Neuengamme, the Nazi industrial complex of Watenstedt/ Salzgitter, November 3, 1944 (Appendix A). Salzgitter is approximately 314 kilometers (195 miles) southwest of Ravensbrück, equivalent to a present-day three-hour car drive. The travel was likely by rail, freight cars with very crowded conditions as described earlier, with many delays for military rail traffic. Based on other accounts of prisoner transport, the trip could have taken days. It is unlikely that water or food was provided.

Watenstedt was one of many satellite camps of Neuengamme. The first female prisoners were transported to Watenstedt/Leinde from Ravensbrück Concentration Camp in July 1944 (KZDrütte). Over time, the number of women detained at Watenstedt rose to 1,500. Most of the prisoners were active members of the Resistance. When nearby satellite camps were dissolved, the population increased to unknown numbers.

Living conditions in these Nazi work camps were extremely harsh. The prisoners' clothing, sanitary conditions, and food were insufficient, and the physical work was hard. The people experienced many accidents and diseases. The infirmary was overcrowded and there was a shortage of medical supplies, medicine, and medical personnel. Many deaths occurred (KZDrütte) (Zacharias).

Margit wrote a barely legible postcard from Watenstedt to Margot. The only cards that could be mailed had to be written in the German language with no blotting out or erasing information. They were not allowed to write about the conditions of the camp (Zacharias). In the postcard, Margit sends her regards to Margot's family and asks for them to tell her Oma where she is. She specifically requested that bouillon, bread, and onions be sent to her. She said they do not have much food to eat. She does not complain about any of the conditions at the camp. The card has a stamp on it with the postmark of Watenstedt. A picture of the card is included in Appendix A. Margot's family was not able to send any food to Margit, nor was Margit's Oma able to send any food. Both families were probably on rations and received only enough food for themselves to live.

Margot told me that her father became very upset and fearful when he saw the postcard. If the Gestapo became aware of a family's association with a Jewish person, they, too, might have to go to a camp. He told Margot to throw the card away. But Margot hid the card under her bed mattress. This was very brave for Margot to do at twelve years old. Margot gave the card to Hugo when he returned from the war, hoping that he would start the process of looking for her friend.

One of the few stories my mom told me about her captivity at the camp was that she had to clean the commander's office. When she cleaned his office, he would leave one slice of bread in his top drawer for her. Margit told us that she believed that is how she survived starvation while at the camp.

During my 2014 visit to the Neuengamme Memorial site I had an opportunity to visit with the director, Dr. Reimer Möller. When he saw the postcard that Margit sent, he knew that Margit had been a prisoner at Watenstedt rather than at the main Neuengamme Camp. I also related the story Margit had told my siblings and I about cleaning the commander's office and the slice of bread left in the drawer. Upon hearing this, he became very animated and said that he knew exactly who this commander was. Tom and I, both speechless, glanced at each other with amazement. Dr. Möller ushered us into his office to explain.

The commander who Margit was referring to was Captain Theodor Johann Breuing. It turned out that Captain Breuing had his own tragic story, and in fact, someone wrote a book about him. Captain Breuing was an older man, drafted against his choice into the SS, and therefore had conflicts with his hard-line SS non-commissioned officers. Toward the end of the war, he had to supervise the evacuation of the prisoners from Watenstedt/Salzgitter. The prisoners were put on a train to the Bergen-Belsen concentration camp but got redirected to Ravensbrück. In the chaos surrounding the closing period of the war, he lost track of the prisoners and was unable to account for them. He was arrested by his fellow SS troops. Within a week, and with his entire battalion present, he was executed by firing squad for neglecting his duties. A summary of his story as provided by Dr. Möller is in Appendix C.

To this day, my discovery of the connection between my mother and Captain Breuing gives me chills. First of all, I can't even imagine what Margit would have felt if she knew that I had found the commander who saved her life. But even more profoundly, it brought to light that even in the darkest hours, one person in a Nazi uniform who each day made decisions of life and death chose to show a small kindness amid the cruelty. I obviously can't thank him for that, but I hope that my relating of this story will give everyone a reason to remember him as a man of compassion in a most perilous time.

Unlike my mother, some former concentration camp survivors were eager to tell their stories after the war. One of these was Maria Stanislwaw, a woman who was also a prisoner at Watenstedt/Salzgitter camp during the same time as Margit. She gave the following testimony in Sweden at a postwar inquiry:

This camp was an ammunition factory. The women worked in the factory to make bullets for light cannons. The work was hard, standing twelve hours at a time. Weak women fainted of exhaustion. When leaving morning time for the factory they would stand in roll call for an hour. The same repeated in the evening. They worked one week during the day and the next one during the night. Initially the food was very bad: vegetables and some potatoes, a quarter of a bread loaf. After two weeks the food improved because we couldn't work; they gave a little better soup and more bread. Twice a week, they received 1 kg (2.2 pounds) of bread for three and four times a week. One had to make 1,500 bullets (5 kg) daily. There were many injuries and accidents at work, injuring fingers and burning hands, legs and faces. They had to walk barefooted. The female supervisors were very mean, they didn't allow women to go to the bathroom, the women were sick and they couldn't go out. They relieved themselves at the machines, for which they were beaten.

It was dirty in the blocks and there were many lice. Blankets were taken to be deloused but returned full of lice. On January 7, 1945, the women were ordered to take everything including blankets and were driven 5 km to the bath, with sanitizing chambers for belongings. They bathed without soap and beaten when someone couldn't clean herself sufficiently.

On January 14, 1945, there was a huge air raid. American bombs bombed all the factories around. They survived but the work in the factories was terminated. They were held in blocks for 3 days. The Aufsehers (supervisors) carried out long and strict searches. There were approximately 800 prisoners of various nationalities. After those 3 days they were taken out of the camp and cleaned the railroad tracks and tidied things, this lasted 3 weeks. Later they put stalls under canopies and they demanded that prisoners work, but the work didn't progress, the end was in sight. This lasted until April 7.

On April 7 at 8:00 a.m. prisoners were called out from the blocks to undergo another evacuation. They stood with their belongings for 2 hours. Everyone was ordered to return back to his or her blocks. After an hour, they were marched out again with all their belongings. In groups of 100, they went through the gate escorted by drunken SS men. They boarded a freight train in wagons under heavy escort. They travelled 7 days. The train consisted of 90 wagons overcrowded with people, 80-90 in every wagon. Bread was provided through 5 days in 6 portions with a small amount of margarine. Water was acquired at the stops. During the trip there were air raids almost every evening, the train was machine gunned, killing 40 persons. Many people died during the trip. The train always stood between *the military trains. During the air raids SS ran away first and we sat often in locked wagons. If someone moved SS guards threatened to shoot. They guarded the prisoners from a distance with rifles in their hands. They arrived in Ravensbrück April 23.*

*But once more the prisoners were forced to walk, a death march for many, in the direction west because the Soviet Army was near Ravensbrück from the east. They walked 3 days, slept in a forest for the first two nights, anyone that faltered was shot dead. The third day they reached the small concentration camp of Malchow, a sub-camp of Ravensbrück about 70 kilometers away. The next morning the prisoners got up and walked out of the barracks and stood there to be counted—like every day before. But there were no guards anymore. The Germans disappeared in the night. Near the camp were some farms and we went there to get some food.*

This account was provided by Elke Zacharias, director of the KZ Denke/Drütte Memorial Center ("KZ" is a German abbreviation of concentration camp), with translation by Roman Solecki on January 14, 2014.

I never realized that Margit had to endure a death march until I read the above account in 2015. She never mentioned it. I asked Director Zacharias if it was possible Margit was, in fact, on the death march. She assured me that from everything we know from Margit's records, and the story I told her about Margit's liberation (told below), that she most certainly was evacuated from the Ravensbrück Concentration Camp and would have been among those marching in the death march. Once more the reality of what Margit suffered, and yet was able to carry on with her life, struck my heart.

Margit told me that she knew that if the war had not ended when it did, she would have died. She said she was so sick that she would have been sent to the gas chambers. She related to my siblings and I that the camp prisoners were not liberated directly by one of the Allied armies or Russian armies, which comports with Maria's testimony. She also told me that "they woke up that morning, stood in line to be counted, but the guards were gone."

Eva Timar, another prisoner in the Watenstedt/Salzgitter Camp, gave this testimony (Petrovic):

*In Bergen Belsen we use to get soup once a day but there were no gas chambers like in Auschwitz. There was no endless counting there, it was a surprisingly calm period but in mid-December we were transported from there to clean the derelict houses in Brauschweig where it was terrible. There were about 300 women. We used to clean the derelict houses the entire winter under terrible conditions of famine, cold, disease, lice, and from there I was transported to the camp hospital in Wattenstedt. This saved me as I recovered somewhat there and at the beginning of April Wattenstedt was evacuated and I reached Ravensbrück where women from all over the world were kept who were brought from various camps. Terrible conditions, no food. From there we started the so called death march because people were dying all the time, weakened, sick. After four days of marching I arrived to Malchow camp where the next day, on May 2, 1945, a year after my arrival to Auschwitz, the Red Army liberated us. I was extremely weak and sick, without hair, coughing I barely dragged myself. I had a number on my arm which I still have—80692. We were liberated in a mental state of apathy. They gathered all of us in a collection camp for Yugoslav people. Until, there walked from Malchow or went by train…*

Margit had been in detention and concentration camps from August 1944 through April 27, 1945, consuming over nine months of her early teenage years. The directors of the Holocaust memorial sites that we visited all expressed surprise at how young Margit was at the time and said that she would have been one of the youngest prisoners in the work camps. Based on the testimony of fellow prisoners, she certainly saw much brutality, torture, and shockingly horrific things. She chose to block them from her memory. I also believe that she was supported by the care and strength of other women prisoners who fought to survive during their ordeal.

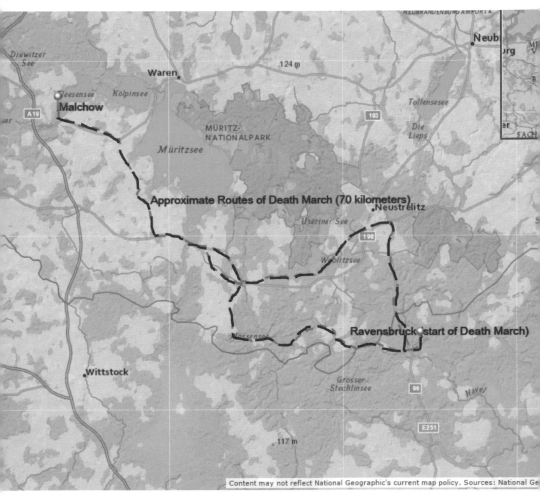

*Map of death march from Ravensbrück to Malchow (dashed lines)*

# CHAPTER FIVE

# End of the War

꧁❀꧂

The survivors of the death march to Malchow awoke to liberation on May 2, 1945. Eva Timar's account illustrates the precarious state of the survivors. She stayed at the Malchow camp and was part of the ensuing rescue operation. But in the initial hours after their Nazi guards disappeared, the survivors must have been on their own.

Margit's own account of this momentous day was about her self-rescue. Filthy and starving, she was able to walk to a farm near the Malchow camp. The farmers took pity on her and took her in. My mother told me that her appearance and body had so degenerated that the farmers did not know if she was male or female. They provided her a portion of what little food they had. Even though the farmers told her to eat slowly and in small amounts until her stomach got used to food again, Margit could not eat anything without throwing up. This and diarrhea continued for days; she was suffering from starvation. Finally, she was able to eat. Margit lived in the farmers' barn and worked for them for approximately eight months, regaining her strength. It is my understanding that the farmers found or arranged for someone who was transporting people back to their homes in what was occupied West Germany.

In the immediate aftermath of World War II, the four main allies in Europe—the United States, Great Britain, the Soviet Union, and France—took part in a joint occupation of Germany. This arrangement divided Germany into four zones of occupation. The borders of these zones were never entirely sealed, but there were severe restrictions on the movements of the German citizens (U.S. Department of State). The border could be crossed legally only through a limited number of routes. River crossings were subject to inspections and restrictions.

Margit was deeply grateful to these farmers for the rest of her life. I remember her writing to them on a regular basis, and she sent packages to them when I was growing up. Unfortunately, I do not have the address or names of these generous people. When I visited Malchow in May 2016, I walked down the country road (Lagerstraße) leading from the former camp to the surrounding farms, trying to imagine where she could have gone. At a meeting arranged by the mayor of Malchow, I told this story to a news reporter who was going to write and publish an article that, hopefully, would help identify these farmers or their descendants.

Unfortunately, the horror of Margit's fifteenth year had not ended following her survival and rescue by the farmers. Her friend, Margot Turner, told me the rest of the story as told to her by Margit.

Margit was one of eight people to be transported or smuggled by a man to the western zone. During the journey they came to a large river, which, based on the geography of the area, might have been the Elbe. The man took everyone over the river but Margit. He had told her to wait for him and that he would take her across later. When he returned, he told her if she wanted to go any further she must submit to him sexually. Although Margit refused, the man insisted and raped Margit several times before he took her across (Turner).

Finally, in December 1945, on her own, Margit arrived at the old apartment in Frankfurt, Germany, that she previously shared with her Oma and Hugo prior to her imprisonment. Postwar documents revealed that 65 percent of the city was destroyed or damaged by Allied bombing and artillery (Stanley). She saw a bombed-out shell of a city, with devastation replacing the splendor that was prewar Frankfurt.

Margit only told this final story segment of her return to her home in Frankfurt to her friend Margot. She approached the doorstep and rang the doorbell, not sure if her family still lived there. She was filthy dirty and had lice; her hair was still very short. Hugo, her Oma, and her father's new girlfriend must have been very surprised to see her when she opened the door. But instead of hugging her and saying that they were so happy to have her back home, they shuttled her to the basement washroom. Her Oma and her father's new girlfriend, Hallie, stripped Margit's clothes off of her and hosed her down with water! Margit told Margot she was utterly humiliated by the entire experience. She was stripped naked in her own home in front of a woman she didn't know. This treatment must have evoked unpleasant memories from the concentration camps.

# CHAPTER SIX

# Returning Home

Returning home to their native Germany was hard on the Jewish people who survived the war. Other Jewish survivors, including Viktor E. Frankl, who wrote the book, *Man's Search for Meaning*, wrote about this subject. They were not welcomed back with apologies and sorrow for all their suffering, but with an attitude of "we too suffered" during the war. There was disillusionment for many Jews, which was very difficult or impossible to overcome (Frankl).

Mr. Frankl wrote:

> *But for every one of the liberated prisoners, the day comes when, looking back on his camp experiences, he can no longer understand how he endured it all. As the day of liberation eventually came, when everything seemed to him like a beautiful dream, so also comes the day when all his camp experiences seem nothing to him but a nightmare.*

So, you may wonder as I did for many years, where was Margit's father Hugo, during the eight months she was recovering and attempting to reach home? When the war ended May 8, 1945, Hugo returned home to Frankfurt am Main. He had been a prisoner of war in an American camp. Hugo had served in the Marine Corps on the ship *Stavanger* (Kühner). He wrote in his memoir that when he arrived at Eckenheimer Land Street he was happy to find the apartment where he had lived still standing. The windows were gone but had been boarded up. Inside he found his mother (Oma) in bed, nearly starved to death. But he did not find Margit. Hugo sent a letter to the Central Tracing Bureau looking for her. The bureau only knew that she was listed as missing. Hugo and Oma thought, I believe, that Margit had died, along with the millions of other Jewish people who perished in the concentration camps.

When Margit unexpectedly returned home in December 1945, he was happy, of course. He brought her to the Jewish Consulate where she received new clothes and some money.

She was sixteen years old in February 1946. I know that she went to the American House School to learn English. According to Margot Turner, Hugo, once again attempting to exert control, wanted Margit to marry well. He was hoping to find her a well-to-do Jewish husband. My mother also alluded to this fact; Hugo wanted her to marry a man of money, likely the reason why he never embraced my father.

*Margit in 1946, standing near the rubble of a building that was bombed in Frankfurt during World War II.*

# CHAPTER SEVEN

# Marriage to Angelo Pascetti

&#x2015;&#x2766;&#x2015;

Margit met Angelo Pascetti, a twenty-five-year-old American GI, on one of her walks to or from the American House School. Angelo was a very good-looking Italian American. My mother, recounting the story of their meeting, indicated that it went something like this: Angelo whistled at her and said, "Hey Frauline." Margit was always a friendly person, so I can imagine them striking up a conversation that led to dates—taking walks, going on picnics, and Margit's favorite activity of going to the Palmengarten (botanical garden) in Frankfurt. On January 17, 1948, Margit and Angelo were engaged to be married. Coincidentally, this was the wedding date of Hugo and Hallie.

Angelo, twenty-eight years old, and Margit, nineteen years old, were married January 27, 1949. I was born January 15, 1949, in Frankfurt, Germany, at a German hospital. My birth certificate records my mom as Margit Chinkes, Jewish, and my father as Angelo Pascetti, Catholic. I am a naturalized citizen of the United States of America due to being born of one American parent.

I was rather dismayed when, in high school, I realized my parents were married after my birth date. When I finally got the courage to bring this topic to her attention, my mom told me, "Things were different in those days." She and my dad were married twice, once by the German officials and once by the American officials, both in Frankfurt, Germany. I was only aware of the January 27, 1949, date, which is the one they celebrated as their wedding anniversary.

At the time of their marriage, Angelo was still a soldier in the U.S. Army. His Army unit returned to the United States of America in March 1949, and he separated with an honorable discharge. Angelo returned to Albuquerque, New Mexico, where most of his brothers and sister lived.

Margit had to stay in Germany to acquire the necessary paperwork to travel to the United States of America. This was another very difficult time for her. She had to cope with a brand-new baby by herself, while living with Hallie and Hugo. Just before Angelo left for his home country, her Oma had died.

Margit was a mature nineteen-year-old woman who had already experienced life's worst cruelty and viciousness. It seemed to me that she wanted a new beginning. In a love letter to Angelo, she wrote, "Nothing is here in Germany what could hold me, not even my father is something for me when I could come to you."

*Marriage day of Margit and Angelo,*
*January 27, 1949, Frankfurt, Germany*

After my father died in 2014, I discovered many love letters that Margit wrote to Angelo from March 1949 through June 1949. Margit's written English was very good. The letters have lipstick kisses on them and were always signed with many kisses from your wife (Appendix B). She wrote of the conflict she felt with Hallie and expressed relief when Hallie and Hugo were gone for a few days.

Also included in her letters was news of how I was growing and what I was learning to do. She always called me "the baby." She never called me by name. She took me for many walks in a baby carriage to nearby parks and visited her German friends who had also married American GIs.

Margot Turner told me that Margit had some initial uncertainty about leaving Germany and her father. But as time passed, she became very anxious to leave. Margot said she wanted to get away from the "bad memories of Germany." Also, it was evident from her letters that Margit was concerned about money. She wanted Angelo to find a good, safe job so they could buy a home. In a letter, she requested that Angelo not meet her in New York City when she and I finally arrived but to save the money so they could buy the necessary items for their new life together. Margit worried that Angelo's American family wouldn't approve of him marrying a German girl. That worry was needless as the Pascetti family always accepted and loved Margit as their own family.

My mother and I sailed on the *Marine Shark* departing June 8, 1949, from Hamburg, Germany, to New York City. The *Marine Shark* was a U.S. transport ship operated by the United States Lines. It carried only one class of passengers that originated from various ports. We arrived in New York on June 18, 1949 (Appendix B).

I wonder how she sailed for ten days with a five-month-old infant. I can't imagine the diaper situation (no disposable diapers). In her letters to my dad prior to us leaving, she often spoke of washing diapers and hoping they would dry. I wonder if she got seasick or if she made friends with anyone on the ten-day voyage. I do know that when she arrived in New York a woman befriended her. I believe her name was Dorothy Carrara (I found a postcard addressed to her in Branchton, PA, but there was no note). She helped Margit get train tickets to Chicago, Illinois, and continuing on to Albuquerque, New Mexico. The train ticket to Albuquerque said, "Discharge to Travelers Aid." My dad's sister, Carmen, met my mom and me at the train station (Appendix B). My dad was not there as he was working.

# CHAPTER EIGHT

# Early Life in the United States

⤛❦⤜

After my dad was discharged from the Army, he lived in Albuquerque. Most of his family lived there due to the availability of work in the larger city. Angelo grew up in the coal mining town of Dawson, in northeastern New Mexico, which by then had become a ghost town. Both his parents had died in Dawson while he was in the service. Both he and my mom wanted to be near his family roots and his siblings, but Angelo did not enjoy living in the "big city." So in 1950 when his brother Jack moved to Winton, Wyoming, to work in a coal mine, he followed Jack, bringing Margit and me along.

Winton was a company town, meaning it was a place where the mining company was the employer and owned practically all of the property, stores, and housing. The Union Pacific Coal Company provided infrastructure of the town to enable the workers to live. Winton was fourteen miles north of Rock Springs, Wyoming, at an elevation of 7,000 feet. It was in the "middle of nowhere" then and it still is today. The population ranged from 500 to 700 people. The Union Pacific pulled out in 1953 when there was a shift from coal-fired steam power to diesel-fueled locomotive trains, and coal was replaced with natural gas for residential heating (McLean and Telck). The town quickly vanished and became yet another ghost town like Dawson.

In Margit's love letters to Angelo, she had asked him to get a safe job. She undoubtedly had some anxiety and fear of my dad working in the mines, but at the same time, it was her nature to be supportive and to go wherever he went.

Margit received a great amount of support from Jack's wife, Liz. Liz frequently helped Margit learn how to cook and encouraged her to try new "American things." Margit had never eaten corn on the cob—corn was for animals in Germany. But she learned to love it. I remembered my parents and Jack and Liz playing cards in the evening. They also took trips together; they once traveled to Yellowstone National Park for a camping trip. Family activities were very important to Angelo and Margit.

Margit wanted to become an American so she could vote. She acquired her naturalization papers on March 17, 1953 (Appendix A). It must have been a very proud moment for her. My sister, Roxana, and my brother, Gerald, were born in Rock Springs, Wyoming. Rock Springs was a somewhat larger town than Winton and there was a hospital there for birthing.

The following portion of this story comes from both my mother and Ruth Grosch. In 1953, Margit received a startling letter from Ruth, who was living in Bad Tennstedt, Germany (see map in Chapter 1). Ruth claimed in the letter that she was Margit's half-sister! Margit could hardly believe the words she saw on paper. She wrote immediately to Hugo, wanting an explanation. Indeed, Hugo admitted to Margit that he did father another child, Ruth. According to Ruth, he didn't have any connection or relationship with Ruth's mother, Clara, subsequent to impregnating her in 1925.

Like Margit's mother, Ruth's mother was left to raise her child on her own. Ruth's Oma, Berta, and her husband raised Ruth. She knew her father's name was Hugo Kühner. She also remembered having a "playdate" with her half-sister, Margit, when Ruth was around seven years old in Erfurt, Germany. Margit was only two years old and, as far as I know, had no memory of the playdate.

One afternoon in 1953, Ruth went to her local beautician who was also a friend. The friend showed her a newspaper article in *Der Spiegel*, a tabloid, about Hugo Kühner. The article called him the greatest swindler in West Germany (Grosch).

What did Hugo do to get this type of notoriety?

Hugo was a professional autograph hunter. He collected signatures from prominent people around much of the world, which were contained in a 160-pound book. He intended to dedicate the signatures to a popular cause— Peace to the World—and it was his stated intent to give the book to the United Nations. The people who signed the book wrote checks to Hugo and he in turn promised to give each person a small copy of the book. Hugo received over 200,000 DM by the time the police got involved. This sum would have been about $50,000 in 1953 (today, more than $450,000). Hugo did not print or distribute small versions of his autograph book nor did he pay taxes or report this income to the government. Most of the money was spent on personal expenses (Kühner). Hugo went to court and was sentenced to two and one-half years of prison, but it is unknown whether he spent any time in jail. His book is reportedly in the archives of the criminal law school in Düsseldorf.

When the article came out, Hugo was living in Frankfurt, Germany, with his wife Hallie. Ruth contacted them. Hugo was very reluctant to provide her with any information about Margit. But eventually, Hallie persuaded him to give her information, including Margit's address in the United States of America, and Hugo had to admit to Margit that she indeed had a half-sister named Ruth.

Ruth and Margit frequently wrote letters to each other. Ruth was living in what was East Germany, known as the German Democratic Republic (GDR). I remember my mom mailing Christmas packages to Ruth and her family for years. The half-sisters did not meet until Ruth and her son and his family came to this country in 1993, four years after the fall of the Berlin Wall.

Ruth and Margit found that their lives had many parallels. Hugo abandoned both of their mothers during their pregnancies. Their Omas raised both of the girls, as their mothers could not manage parenting without support. Also, both women married men who were nine years older than they were. And even more amazing, each sister named her firstborn daughter Angelika! It gave me the chills when Ruth provided this information to me.

When the coal mine in Winton, Wyoming, closed down in 1953, my dad was forced to look for other work. We moved back to Albuquerque where dad's siblings still lived. He took a job at a furniture store. Dad always wanted to provide for his family and did what it took to give us a home. But once again, he did not enjoy living in Albuquerque. His brother Jack found a mining job in a molybdenum mine near Leadville, Colorado. Work seemed stable, so my parents moved to Leadville in 1954. Angelo took a job working for Climax Molybdenum for $1.75 per hour. Today, this wage would be $15.63 per hour.

They found a small rental near Jack and Liz's home but wanted to own a home. Across the street was an abandoned home with two bedrooms and no indoor plumbing. They decided to buy it and paid $600.00 cash for their "new" home! In 2016, this is approximately $5,358.00.

Leadville is the highest incorporated city in the United States of America, at 10,152 feet above sea level, and for this reason, it is also one of the coldest cities.

I remember the well in the front yard and the outside toilet. I hated to go outside to the bathroom in the winter. I remember vividly the outhouse throne with two holes. Roxie, my sister, lost her favorite toy down one of the holes when we were playing. It was a green rubber dog named Pluto with a bulb that when you squeezed it, it moved. The kitchen, which later became my sister and my bedroom, had a woodstove for cooking.

Mom and Dad were proud of their home and started work on it immediately! They did the work themselves and paid for it as they went along. They made it into a three-bedroom home, doubled the size of the living room, installed a modern kitchen, and best of all, put in up-to-date plumbing! My parents dug out a basement under the new living room by hand. Its walls were dirt their entire lives. Mom grew a garden and flowers in the spacious yard that surrounded the house. She loved her flowers and grew everything she could in Leadville's short growing season.

My Uncle Jack and his family left Leadville in 1958 when workers at the Climax mine went on strike. They were on strike from July through October of that year. Jack no longer wanted to deal with the uncertainty of mining. But my parents persisted; they were not willing to leave Leadville where they were trying to make a home.

They survived the first strike, but in 1962 workers at the mine went on strike again—this time it was from July 18, 1962, through January 1963. I remember that as a difficult time for my parents. But what I remember most is that I was never hungry! My mom learned to cook the commodities she obtained—canned meat and other items. I'm sure my dad hunted, and to this day I don't like deer meat, as we must have eaten a lot of it. I remember that my dad had to stand in the strike line; he got paid $15.00 per day just for doing that.

My dad finally was forced to look for work elsewhere. He again went to Albuquerque. We must have spent Christmas 1962 in Albuquerque. I don't remember feeling poor or sad or hungry during that time or any time of my childhood.

When the strike ended, my dad returned to the Climax mine and worked there until he retired in 1983. He worked at Climax as a miner for twenty-nine years. My mom never doubted my dad nor do I remember her complaining about my dad's working situation. She always supported him in every way she could.

My mom finally was able to take a trip to her beloved Germany when I was sixteen years old in 1965. It was the first time my parents could afford to take such a trip. Margit had not seen her father since she left him in Hamburg, Germany, in 1949. My dad did not accompany us on the trip. It was mom and me and my two siblings, Roxie and Gerald. It was a very exciting trip for us. It was our first time on an airplane; we flew on Lufthansa Airlines with a German club from Denver. The flight was very festive—people singing German songs and drinking.

None of us kids knew what to expect from our grandparents, Hugo and Hallie. They never really felt like grandparents, as we never saw them and all their letters to Margit were in German so we couldn't read them. Hugo at that time owned a German wine restaurant, the Southern Star.

Hugo and Hallie didn't know what to do with us either. The first thing they did was to buy dresses for my sister and me. They were simple polyester dresses that were beige in color with dark brown trim. Neither Roxie nor I liked the dresses, but we were forced to wear them everyplace we went with Hugo and Hallie. I can't remember what Gerald had to wear, but I'm sure it was a similar drab outfit. My grandparents liked Gerald with his crew cut hair—they called him a "little porcupine."

Because they ran their restaurant business and stayed up late, we were expected to be quiet when they were sleeping in the morning. It was not an easy thing to do when you're sixteen, fourteen, and twelve years old. The apartment was above the restaurant. One evening Gerald was curious about the restaurant and decided that he wanted to peek at it. So he climbed up on a skylight on the roof and fell through the glass. Luckily Gerald wasn't hurt badly, but he got into major trouble. We never became comfortable with Hallie or Hugo and actually were happy to return home to Leadville.

Mom and Dad traveled back to Germany on a regular basis after us children left home. Hugo and Hallie came to the United States of America two times for a visit after that. I don't think any of us kids thought they were happy visits; it was always stressful, especially for my dad.

In the fall of 1973 my mom and I went to Germany together. It was a wonderful trip especially since it was just the two of us! However, even though I had been living on my own since 1970, when I graduated from my nursing training, my mom still wanted to take care of me. She even held my hand crossing the street! We had so much fun exploring and eating our way through Germany. In one entry of her travel journal, she wrote, "Our trip to the Saalburg castle brought back memories of '46-47. It's been that long since I walked 8 kilometers in one stretch."

I now wonder what memories those were for her. The Saalburg is a Roman fort between Bad Hamburg and Wehrheim, Germany. In her little diary of our trip, my mom recorded all of the restaurants that we went to. She wrote down the specific foods that we ate and the coffee or wine that we drank.

During our trip to Germany we took a bus tour to Paris, France. Mom easily made friends on the three-day tour. We visited all of the tourist stops, including the Eiffel Tower, a river tour down the Seine, and Castle Versailles.

Before we left Germany we visited one more time with our new friends to say good-bye. When we returned to Denver, Colorado, she ended her journal with this note, "Now our everyday life can begin again. It will be nice to be home with such beautiful memories."

My mom and dad made several trips back to Germany after 1973. Her goal was to return to Germany every other year. She was always very happy to return to her homeland. On one such trip, my mom, dad, and his sister, Carmen, ventured to Italy. Mom was determined to find and meet my dad's Italian family. She had done her research on the family and discovered where they lived. There was little contact between my mom and the Italian family, but it was decided to rent a car and visit them anyway. My parents and my aunt drove from Germany through northern Italy to Rome and then east to the small town of San Valentino de Abruzo.

I believe some members of dad's family were skeptical as to whether or not my dad was really related to the family in San Valentino until my dad and his cousin, Nicola, stood next to each other. The family resemblance was obvious. The visit was beyond everyone's expectations—my dad, his sister, my mom, and the new-found family. I believe it was one of the highlights of my dad's life. I know it was for his sister, Carmen! My mom was absolutely thrilled to see how this family was living off their farm.

The region of Germany where Margit's half-sister, Ruth Grosch, and her family lived was liberated by Allied Forces. But it was later relinquished to Russian occupation and became part of the Communist bloc. The infamous Berlin Wall was built in 1961; the fencing and guard towers were extended along the east-west boundary to prevent movement of people from the Eastern bloc to Western Europe. The wall became a tangible symbol of human oppression.

In 1989, people on both sides of the Berlin Wall took the wall down to make Germany united again. For the first time since World War II, the ability for the East Germans to travel freely to West Germany was a reality.

In 1993, Ruth, after living the postwar years in East Germany, was finally able to travel to the West. Margit welcomed Ruth, her son, Wolfgang, and his wife, Edeltraud, along with one of their children, to her home in Leadville. Since 1953 Margit and Ruth had exchanged letters and pictures, but they were both overjoyed to finally meet each other in person! It was an exciting time for Margit and Ruth to get acquainted in this country. My mom and dad brought Ruth and family to see my brother, Gerald, in Hayden, Colorado. They traveled to Billings, Montana, where Roxie and I were making our home. We all traveled to Yellowstone Park, packing in as much adventure as we could. It was a wonderful trip in addition to a very happy time for my mom and Ruth.

# CHAPTER NINE

# Cancer

⟿❦⟾

In the fall of 1994, Margit slipped and fell at the grocery store in Leadville. She did not go to the doctor immediately, as she was sure her pain on her side was nothing. But when it did not go away for weeks, she sought medical attention. An x-ray was done of her chest, looking for perhaps a broken rib or pneumonia. But instead, the physician found a suspicious spot on her right lung. It needed to be biopsied. The biopsy determined that Margit had malignant melanoma. It was not the primary lesion but a secondary site, meaning that the melanoma had spread from another site in her body. A Denver surgeon wanted to remove the lesion by removing my mother's lung.

As a nurse, I knew that just removing the lung was not going to cure my mom's cancer. My sister and I drove to Leadville that December. I explained to Margit that she needed a second opinion before she underwent such a radical surgery. We asked our parents to come to Billings so we could be support for them during this difficult time. They agreed to come, so we assisted in arranging the necessary doctor appointments. The news was not good. The malignant melanoma diagnosis was confirmed. Surgery was not the answer. Margit would have to undergo chemotherapy.

The doctor did not give us much hope. He said Margit would probably only have one year to live even with treatment. The chemotherapy was harsh, and Margit needed to take it every four weeks. Mom and Dad thought it was best if she took the chemotherapy in Billings and live with my sister, Roxie, or me. They initially stayed with Roxie, but later moved into my house as her health deteriorated. They returned to their Leadville home in between cycles of chemotherapy as they could. Her hair thinned but she never lost all of it. She became weak, was very nauseated, and vomited a great deal. This was the first time since her post-concentration camp time that she was not able to eat, even though she wanted to.

Margit's medical routine ruled all our lives. After each cycle of treatment she needed another CAT scan to see if the treatment was doing its job of shrinking the tumors. It was always stressful, because if the chemotherapy was not working, then it would be the end of treatment.

Margit did have some good days between the treatments. She enjoyed small outings and the visitors who came to see her. On one outing we went to Crow

Fair on the Crow Indian Reservation about sixty-five miles southeast of Billings. Margit was her old self, wanting to take pictures of the Native American dancers in their colorful beaded outfits. On another day she had the energy to make her German bread, making the house smell wonderful.

In the middle of September 1995 we received the CAT scan report that we dreaded—the chemotherapy was no longer working. Margit's tumor load had tripled in volume. Her doctor gave her the option of taking another chemotherapy, Interferon, a biological used as an immune-regulator to inhibit cellular growth. Margit did not have much hope in it, as it was only a small injection. She couldn't understand how a "small shot" could be effective.

Margit had her final CAT scan on November 13. Cancer was in her liver, lung, spine, and ribs, and one could feel the tumors on her left leg and on the top of her scalp. The cancer had taken over her body.

My mom and dad were living with Tom and me. We knew it would not be long before Mom would be gone. We initiated hospice care. Margit was alert and still able to do her own care, but on November 21 she started bleeding, making her very weak. Her pain was extreme and very difficult to control, especially when she moved. We got a hospital bed to help make her more comfortable. Finally, the pain medication was effective. On the night of November 24 we all took shifts being with Mom. We played her German music and read to her.

Margit died on November 25, 1995, around 11:43 A.M., with all her children and her husband in the room.

The cancer shattered Margit's dreams. She never expected to die before my dad, much less at sixty-five years old. I believe she thought she would return to Germany to live out her life after my dad passed.

I loved my mom very much. I'm thankful we had her last year of life together to share. It was not easy, but I got to know my mom and dad again as parents. They got to know Tom and me along with their grandchildren, Julianna and Amber, who were still at home. There was some good and some bad in that year, but we were together as family.

# CHAPTER TEN

# Reflections

◈

Margit did not go to church, but she made sure all of her children were baptized in the Catholic faith, as my dad was Catholic. She wanted all of us to receive the sacraments of the church—communion, confirmation, and marriage—in the church, which we did. She attended all of our religious ceremonies. When she knew she was going to die, she requested to be cremated and not to be buried in the Catholic Church. As a child who loves her parent, her requests were honored even though it was painful for me at the time.

Although Margit did not practice a religion, she did believe in God. She had a strong inner resolve; I can only surmise that it came from God.

My mother's life was full of challenges. She was very close to death early in her life. She accepted those challenges without self-pity, always with hope and belief in a better life. She always tried to face up to each situation with dignity and fortitude. Margit never wanted to be defined by her Holocaust experience but simply as another war survivor and immigrant who lived her life loving her family. She did whatever it took to care for us. She was tenacious in learning new skills and adapting to new situations. I have learned much about my mom, perhaps more after her death than when she was alive.

# CHAPTER ELEVEN

# Finding the "Lost Family"

⌀

Fast forward to 2015. I've spent months doing research, looking at documentation of my mother and her life, but I still had a missing piece of the puzzle that needed to be explored. Margit made one trip to Vienna with Angelo after all of her children had left home. I assumed she went there because it was her birthplace, but I don't remember her saying she wanted to explore her Chinkes family roots. She never looked for Frieda's family to our knowledge.

Whatever happened to Frieda Chinke's family? Did they escape the Nazi terror or did they die in some concentration camp? I could not find a death certificate for Marjem Flanzgraben, Frieda's mother. I did find the death certificate of Izaak Flanzgraben, Marjem's second husband, in the Jewish Vienna archives. There was no information on Marjem, other than that she was sent to the "re-settlement camp" of Kielce in February 1941. It appeared from the Vienna city archives that she did not return to Vienna.

In November 2015 I traveled to Washington, D.C. to visit my close Jewish friend. Also I wanted to visit the United States Jewish Holocaust Museum. My goal was to visit with a support person in the museum to see if there was additional information on Marjem. I brought what little information I had to the museum.

The museum reference coordinator was most helpful. She looked at the vast bank of computer information available to her, searching for Marjem's name. Success! She pulled up a picture of Marjem and documentation from the Israel Yad Vashem site. Yad Vashem in Hebrew means "museum of martyrs." It is the Jewish people's living memorial to the Holocaust, located in Jerusalem, Israel. I was so excited to see the picture of Marjem! My deeper joy, which I barely dared to hold, was that the mere existence of this document meant that some family member could have survived. It was the first indication that anyone of Frieda's family may have survived the Holocaust.

The certificate, which was written entirely in Hebrew, was translated for me by the museum archivist. It indicated that Marjem's daughter, Shoshanna (Shuli) Atterman, provided the information for the museum in about 1985. Shuli lived in an Israeli kibbutz called Gesher. The coordinator tried to make a phone call to Israel to Shuli, but we were unable to get an answer. But I wasn't about to let that small setback deter me.

*Marjem (Kuj) Flanzgraben*
*Photo from Yad Vashem memorial site*

I returned home and tried the phone number again. No answer. I was willing to try one more gamble. My sister-in-law, Patti Solveson, had been living in Jerusalem on and off for several years. She was an artist who had been painting a mural depicting the major scenes of the Old and New Testaments of the Bible on a 100-meter-long wall in a Christian cemetery. I decided to email her and ask if she was willing to visit this kibbutz to see if she could find Shuli. It was a long shot, as I wasn't sure how far from Jerusalem the kibbutz was located or if she could even get in. Patti was willing! I could only wait and see what happens.

Patti sent me an email several weeks later after a trip that she took to Gesher kibbutz. She had news for me. The kibbutz manager had told her that unfortunately, Shuli had died in 2011, but she had a daughter who lived in another kibbutz. After much explanation and translation Patti was able to speak to Shuli's daughter, Tirza. Tirza said she was willing to email me if I emailed her. So I emailed Tirza immediately after getting Patti's information. I wasn't sure what to expect, but I told myself to wait patiently to hear back.

My wait was not long. That same day I received an email from Hava Feary, a sister of Tirza's who lived in England. Hava asked if we could Skype, but amid the excitement of the moment I couldn't get Skype to work on my computer, so I said I would be willing to talk via phone. I emailed back my phone number. Within minutes, Hava called with several other people on a speaker phone. It was loud with much laughing going on in the background.

Of course there were questions. The big one was how did I find them? Did I have a picture of my mom? I thought it was a funny question to ask. I said, "Of course I have a picture of my mom, what do you mean?" Hava said, "Well, we have a picture of her too, when she was a baby." She described the photograph they had, and OH MY, it was the same picture I have of my mom at eight months old. We had the proof that we were indeed related! Our lost families had been reunited after eighty-five years, which included the rise and fall of Nazism, the Holocaust of the Jews, World War II, and a couple of subsequent generations.

A flurry of emails was then exchanged. Frieda had a half-sister, Jenny Rosie, living in Stockholm, Sweden. She was ninety-one years old. I knew immediately I wanted to meet her. I had so many questions. Rosie had two children, Eva Gluckman and Michael Goldstein, who also live in Stockholm. Another exchange of emails ensued. Everyone had questions. Everyone was excited.

Of course I was curious about how the family survived the Holocaust. Through our conversations I discovered that Marjem sent two daughters, Berta and Shoshanna, to Israel in 1938. Two boys, Herman and Jacob, had already been detained in 1939 and sent to the Dachau Concentration Camp. But at that time it apparently was possible to buy your way out. After Marjem paid to have them released, they went to England because they needed to leave Vienna quickly.

*My "lost family," the Flanzgraben family and spouses (left to right):*
*Nicoleta Goldstein, Eva Gluckman, David Feary, Michael Goldstein, Hava Feary,*
*and the author, Angelica Osborne, Stockholm, Sweden, April 2016.*

Rosie was sent to Sweden to work in a Jewish co-op in 1939. Marjem had done whatever it took to save her children. But, it was by then too late for her to escape. As noted on the Yad Vashem document, she was sent to the resettlement camp of Kielce in 1941 where she perished.

Tom and I already knew we were going to travel to Salzgitter, Germany, in April 2016 for a memorial service at the concentration camp that Margit was in. We decided to tack on the trip to Stockholm for what I considered a visit of a lifetime.

We started our much anticipated journey on April 5, 2016, at 7:20 A.M. from Billings, Montana via Seattle, Reykjavik, Iceland, and Frankfurt, Germany, to Stockholm. It took about thirty hours of travel including layovers. We were exhausted when we arrived at our hotel in Stockholm that was in the Soderbalm section of the city, not far from where Eva and Rosie lived. Our hotel was the former queen's hunting chalet. It was old, but charming and quaint. The staff there offered us a wonderful breakfast every morning. Eva came to our hotel in the morning for introductions. She graciously offered to give us a walking tour of the old city of Stockholm; it is a beautiful city built on an archipelago of many islands and waterways. We enjoyed a nice visit together, ending with a delicious lunch of fish chowder.

In the evening we were invited to Eva's home for dinner. Eva's brother, Mickey, and his wife, Nicoleta, were also invited. We were surprised and very happy that David and Hava Feary from England had made the trip to Stockholm to meet us. We enjoyed a long pleasant evening in the warm company of our no-longer-lost family. But we were told that, unfortunately, Rosie was experiencing an acute episode of back pain. Her ability to visit with us was questionable.

We spent five days in Stockholm. Though the weather is not ideal at this latitude in April, we did some great sightseeing and had more meetings and meals with our Jewish family. On the morning of our final day there, I was finally allowed to visit with Rosie in the hospital. The visit was very brief and not the one I dreamed of. There were few answers to the many questions that I had about Frieda. One of my biggest hopes was to see a photo of Frieda, but Rosie had no photos of her.

Nevertheless, I was thrilled to meet Rosie's children and Shuli's daughter, Hava, and her husband. We were warmly welcomed and accepted as family. We were at last reconnected with my grandmother's family after so many years and so much tragedy. I hope to continue the relationships and to incorporate Jewish traditions in my Catholic Christian life. I hope my grandchildren will share my enthusiasm for this exciting new dimension to our lives.

# The Story Behind the Story

⟨◈⟩

Margit died in November 1995. Mother's Day 1996 I decided I would write my mother's story as I knew it. Of course, I wrote it as a nurse writes her nursing entries, just the facts, nothing more. I realized even then that I only had a sparse and incomplete outline. In fact, it took up less than one typewritten page. I knew my mom was fourteen years old when she was imprisoned in two different camps, but where the second camp was located was uncertain. I also knew the story about the gypsy who read her fortune, telling her she wasn't going to die in the camps. In addition, I was aware that she cleaned the commander's office and received a slice of bread in his top desk drawer. Furthermore, I knew she walked away from a camp to a farm at the end of the war and how much she appreciated the farmer's generosity. I was doing the writing for myself, as part of my healing process.

The year 1999 was a big one for our family. Tom and I celebrated our twenty-fifth wedding anniversary. We both recently turned fifty years of age. Our son, Lucas, graduated from the U.S. Air Force Academy, our middle child, Julianna, turned twenty-one years old, and our youngest daughter, Amber, graduated from high school. It seemed like the year to do something "big" as a family. Everyone knew this could be our last chance. We asked the children to weigh in on what they wanted to do, and a wide array of possibilities were discussed. Tom and I were a little surprised when the kids passed on exotic vacation destinations for a trip to Europe, specifically to Germany and Italy where extended family lived.

We all flew out of Denver a couple days after the graduation ceremonies at the Air Force Academy in the first week of June. In Germany we visited Ruth Grosch and her grown children, Angelika and Wolfgang, who lived in or near Bad Tennestedt. We had not seen them since 1993 when they came to visit us in the United States. As always, we enjoyed their whole-hearted hospitality and the wonderful German food and drink.

Bad Tennestedt is approximately forty-two kilometers (twenty-six miles) from the Buchenwald Concentration Camp. We felt that it was a very important place for us to visit, but when we asked if Wolfgang would take us, he initially declined. We Americans are often insensitive to the lingering pain that topics related to World War II bring to the German people.

Finally, Wolfgang agreed to drive and accompany us to the Buchenwald memorial site. He did not go into the memorial concentration camp site but waited outside while we examined and toured the concentration camp. It was very sobering for all of us. After seeing the room with all the shoes, I could hardly believe anyone could have survived the concentration camps. I was also angry. I couldn't understand why, during the war, the German people had turned a blind eye to the concentration camps. The memorial site described how the ovens were manufactured locally in Weimar. Hundreds of local people would have been involved in the construction, servicing, and operation of the camp.

I began to think of what my mom had endured. It also planted the seed for me to visit Ravensbrück Concentration Camp, where I knew she had been sent. But we were not able to make that visit on this trip and didn't return to Germany until 2011.

Wolfgang and I corresponded frequently leading up to the 2011 trip. I told him that I wanted to go to Ravensbrück. I was very happy when he said he would take Tom and I for the visit. I think he was sympathetic that I needed healing. In fact, when we arrived at Ravensbrück, Wolfgang took over and tried to arrange an English-speaking tour. The staff told him it couldn't be done for such a small group. I was so impressed with Wolfgang and appreciated his kind gesture.

On our own, we started our walk around the Ravensbrück grounds. Exhibits were distributed among many buildings on the site. We were not paying much attention to what buildings we were going into and inadvertently entered an administrative building that was not open to the public. A staff person came up to us and asked what we were looking for, to direct us to the exhibits. I explained I didn't know we couldn't be there. I also explained my mother had been there as a prisoner. This appeared to get her attention, especially when I added that she was only fourteen years old when she arrived at Ravensbrück. We were introduced to higher-level staff who began to turn some wheels.

We were escorted to the Ravensbrück Memorial archives/library. I provided the librarian with Margit's information. At first she didn't find anything about Margit because I mistakenly gave her last name as Kühner. When we searched on Chinkes, she found my mother on the rolls and when she was admitted. She showed me her concentration camp ID card. Standing there in that place and seeing her record, the gravity of my mother's potential fate struck my heart with melancholy. I realized I was no longer an ordinary tourist in this place.

From the archives, we learned Margit was in the Ravensbrück camp for approximately three weeks before she was transferred to Neuengamme Concentration Camp near Hamburg, Germany. I was surprised by this new revelation. It reinforced just how little I knew about my mother's experience.

We were given a tour of the entire Ravensbrück camp in English. But now I knew that I must visit the second camp. Once more there was not time on this trip to visit the second camp. I went back home with more questions than I arrived with.

In April 2014 I took a spiritual retreat of several days. When the retreat ended, I felt inspired to write my mom's story for our grandchildren, who were nearing school age. Some had already begun reading on their own. I loved reading books to them. I was sure my mom's story would be one of the most powerful stories they would ever read. If I didn't do it, I knew it would be lost. I mentioned it casually to Lucas, our oldest son, who was so enthusiastic and encouraging that I knew it had to be done. I had so many holes to fill in; I really didn't even know where to begin.

Tom and I decided that we needed to go to Vienna, Margit's birthplace, to see if we could find any more details of her or Frieda's life. We also knew that we needed to go to Neuengamme. We decided to make the trip in September-October 2014. My Jewish friend encouraged me to try to attend the Yom Kippur service that would occur during our scheduled time in Vienna.

I made contact with the Jewish Temple Service office in Vienna to get directions to the cemetery in order to visit Frieda's grave. We were able to obtain tickets for the Yom Kippur service. Over the internet we booked a B&B on the edge of the Vienna Old Town District. It was a bit pricey, but Tom and I felt it would allow us to walk to sights and better use the local public transit.

We arrived on the intercity train to the Wien-Meidling Bahnhof station on the southwest side of Vienna in early evening. Next, we had to figure out how to get to our B&B on the far north side of the city using the U-Bahn underground train system, always a challenge for us country folks. It was a long ride around the Ring-Strasse of Old Town. Darkness had fallen by the time we carried our luggage up the stairs of the Schottenring station. Casually, we noticed it was next to the Danube Canal. We hunted and pecked our way the several blocks to the B&B, checked in, and crashed.

In the morning, as usual Tom needed his exercise so he took off for a jog. He told me that he was heading for the canal we spied from our U-Bahn stop. He found the beautiful path along the Danube Canal. He made a mental note of the name of the bridge stamped in the cement buttress to find the trail access for his next jog.

Later that day, sitting in the office of the Jewish archives, Tom, who had been working on his German, noticed that Frieda's death certificate included the name of the bridge from which she had made her suicide jump, the Augarten Brücke—the same bridge that he used to reach the trail that morning. We looked at each other in one of those "God moments." Of all the places we could have gone in Vienna, we had exited the Schottenring U-Bahn station the previous night about 100 meters from where Frieda ended her life.

During our explorations over the next couple days, we found that the Jewish sector of the city was just across the Augarten Bridge. There we found the apartment building Frieda and Hugo (at times) had occupied in the late 1920s and early 1930s. It felt to us, very much strangers and out of place here, a bit like we were being led by a mysterious tour guide to see what we needed to see. It was exhilarating and humbling to us both that we were staying in the neighborhood in which Frieda and her family had lived.

The afternoon before the Yom Kippur service, the staff of the Jewish archives gave us a brief tour of the synagogue. We were told it was damaged during World War II but it was the only synagogue in Vienna to survive the Nazi's vendetta.

Since neither Tom nor I had ever attended any Jewish service, we expressed our concerns to the staff that we wanted to make sure we followed proper protocol. I did not want to offend anyone at this high service. I explained to the director of the Temple service that I was Catholic and not Jewish. She looked at me sternly and told me that I was Jewish! My mother was Jewish, therefore I was Jewish! I could hardly believe my ears. Never once had I considered myself Jewish. I wonder if Mom considered herself Jewish. If she did, she never said it out loud to any of her children.

We attended the very beautiful Yom Kippur service that Thursday evening. It was a privilege for us to attend this holy service. I enjoyed the view from the balcony with the other women. Tom had a row 3 seat 1 ticket, which turned out to be too close for his comfort level.

We then went to the Jewish cemetery where Frieda was buried. We found her plot with the help of the cemetery's caretakers. I was very saddened to see that her gravesite did not have a marker. I felt like we must have been the only people to have ever paid their respects to her. We laid a beautiful heart-shaped flower arrangement on her grave and also placed a stone there, as we had seen other graves with stones on them in keeping with the Jewish tradition.

Our next stop on this journey was to travel via train from Vienna to Berlin. I wanted to visit the Jewish Museum located there. It was a long nine-hour trip. I was thankful for our first-class seat reservation, but first-class was full and the train was overcrowded with people. People jostled for seats; it was musical chairs at every train stop. Children were crying, some people were talking quietly, but mostly it was noisy and we could smell a lot of body odor. The sky was gray and heavy. We had nothing to eat the entire nine-hour trip as the restaurant was so busy that we could never get into the restaurant car; the porter told us to come back later each time we tried.

I thought of Margit's train trip from Frankfurt to Ravensbrück, probably much more crowded and not even a window to look out of. I thought of the anxiety she may have had being a young teenager not knowing where she was going and what would happen next. It must have been overwhelming. Grousing over my own hunger, I thought that Margit's trip must have been the beginning of her slow starvation.

The Jewish history museum did not disappoint us. It's haunting in many aspects. For me, the darkened room that led me into the museum was especially eerie. And then I was suddenly walking unsteadily on clanking metal plates. Looking down, I saw thousands of plates, each with a face representing a Holocaust victim. Tom and I both experienced a deep haunting feeling, aghast at the magnitude of human suffering represented by these "faces," their last cries echoing as the ringing of the metal in the darkness.

We had just two nights in Berlin. Our next destination was Neuengamme. We took the express train to Hamburg, transferred via a local train to Bergedorf, then took a bus to Kurfürstendeicha station and walked to our B&B. I had arranged for an appointment to visit with the director of the memorial site. Dr. Reimer Möller, the director, came to the hall where Tom and I were waiting to see him. He wanted to know why I thought my mother had been imprisoned here; this camp was mostly for men. Since both Margit's prisoner identification card and the postcard indicated she was sent to Neuengamme, we fully expected this is where she was imprisoned. Dr. Möller, however, clarified for us that in fact, Margit had been sent to the Watenstedt sub-camp located near present-day Salzgitter. Tom and I took a long look at each other—our journey of discovery was not over.

Dr. Möller also told us that Margit may have been spared execution as she was only one-half Jewish and at that time the camps needed the labor from the prisoners for the war effort.

But now our dilemma was finding and getting to Salzgitter/Watenstedt. Two teachers from local schools saw us standing in the rain outside Neuengamme and graciously offered to give us a ride back to our B&B. It was heartwarming to hear of their dedication to having their German students experience the memorial and learn of the Holocaust.

The next morning, we caught the local bus and returned to Hamburg. We rushed to the train station, attempting to catch the next train to Hanover. The train crews were on strike the previous night and things were running slow, unusual for Germany, but good for us as we struggled to figure out the next unplanned leg of this search. After our arrival in Hanover several hours later, we jumped on a local train to Salzgitter.

The station was on the edge of town. We had no clue as to where to go next. None of the instructions we got from Dr. Möller or from Google Maps made sense on the ground. We waited for a local bus and the driver suggested which bus to take, but he didn't know of the memorial site. After a thirty-minute ride we disembarked in Salzgitter/Watenstedt. It was about 3:30 P.M. Children and teenagers just out of school were swarming the bus stop. We still had no idea where the memorial site was from there.

After ten minutes or so, I suddenly realized that I had my suitcase but was without my backpack. Panic set in. We guessed that I left it on the bus, which had of course departed, full of students. At that point, after a very long day of travel, lost in the middle of Germany, and Tom asking me what I remembered doing with my backpack, I broke down.

Then, from nowhere, a couple of teenage girls came up to me and asked—in English—what was wrong. I choked out an explanation, and in seconds, one of them asked to borrow Tom's cell phone. They managed to figure out what bus we may have been on and began making calls to the bus company. The dispatcher patched the call through to a bus driver who asked what my lost pack looked like. After a few words from me, he said that he had it. We just had to wait until he completed his round and he'd deliver it. Sure enough, thirty minutes later there it was, passport, credit cards, and all.

We tried everything we could do to thank these two young "angels"; we offered to buy them dinner, coffee, or give them some money. They refused to take anything and said they had to get home. I managed to get their names and learned that she had a Facebook account. We also learned that they were Germans of Turkish descent. Their parents had immigrated years ago to take advantage of the work opportunities of Salzgitter. I tried unsuccessfully for months afterwards to contact them. I began to believe that they really were angels. Finally, I made contact through Facebook and was able to thank them again and learn a bit more about their lives.

By then it was quite late in the day. I told Tom I was through with busses. We knew we had to be close to the Watenstedt memorial site, but we didn't know how to find it. Tom found a taxi down the street and told the driver, as best he could, where we wanted to go. Of course he couldn't even guess at a fare, but we said we'd pay whatever it took. So off we drove, out of Salzgitter into the countryside. The driver evidently had some idea. He radioed his dispatch office and made a couple phone calls from the road, but no memorial site appeared.

Finally, he pulled off the highway and made one more call. Tom and I peered out the window, seeing what appeared to be some kind of mine property. But between us and the mine, we spied some kind of stone monument. Tom jumped out of the taxi and walked over to a stone obelisk fifty feet off the shoulder. After a few moments, he said, "I think this may be it!" And, sure enough, we found the memorial to the factory in which Margit had been forced to work.

With the meter running up who knew how large a tab, we only had time for a few quick photos and a tearful prayer of gratitude. Back in the taxi we returned to Salzgitter. It was an expensive ride, but I didn't care. We had finally found the place.

Looking at a map we discovered that we were now not that far from Bad Tennstedt and my cousin's house. Even though evening was falling, we decided to hop the local train to Nordhausen. I called Wolfgang and he agreed to come pick us up there. We arrived in Nordhausen in less than two hours. Wolfgang, who had to drive at least an hour, met us as soon as he could get there. We were totally exhausted but extremely grateful for Wolfgang's gracious rescue. There was a wonderful dinner when we arrived at his home.

During our search for the Watenstedt memorial I phoned the director, Elke Zacharias. She was on vacation. She wouldn't return to work until after we needed to journey back to the United States. Elke was also disappointed not to meet us, but she told me there was an annual memorial service on April 15. She extended an invitation for us to attend the memorial event in the future. We were not able to attend the service in 2015 but made plans to be there the following year.

Another survivor's daughter, Lidija Petrovic, and I were honored guests at the memorial service in April 2016. I didn't know what to expect, but the service exceeded my greatest expectations. Lidija and I led a procession over a bridge to the steel factory that originated during the Nazi era and still exists. We both laid a dozen white roses at the memorial site with several other bouquets of flowers. Postcards were made depicting the prisoners who were in KZ Drütte and were distributed to the audience. The steel factory administrators have a motto posted in many places today: No Place for Racism. Speeches were given that included the history of the camp. Elke made arrangements for a tour of the Salzgitter Memorial. She had a full itinerary for us that included lunch and dinner with the people who founded the Salzgitter Memorial, and she also scheduled newspaper and TV interviews. Elke and her staff brought us to Ravensbrück for a personal tour; the highlight of the memorial service was going to Malchow where the war ended and Margit walked to the farmers for her liberation.

My mother's story is a torch that I must carry amid the millions of other stories of Holocaust survivors and victims. Learning my mother's story taught me how important it is to practice tolerance. I understand now that we must never forget what happened to the Jewish people or any other population singled out for persecution. We must never become indifferent to a people's plight due to their ethnicity, religion, or color. I hope that throughout my life I will have many opportunities to share this story and convey its lessons to others.

# Bibliography

Chancellor, Magistratsasbteilung 8. "Historical Viennese Registration Material."
  Vienna, October 20, 2014. Archive Retrieval.

Frankl, Viktor E. *Man's Search for Meaning.* Boston: Beacon Press, 2006.

Geburts - Zeugnis. "Birth Certificate Margit Chinkes." Vienna: Matrikelamt Der
  Israelitischen Kultusgemeinde in Wien, February 13, 1930.

Grosch, Ruth. Interview with author. Bad Tennstedt, June 1999.

Kühner, Max Hugo. *The Story of My Life.* Trans. Werner Will. Frankfurt am
  Main: Self, 1989. Autobiography.

KZDrütte, Gedenke-undDokumentationsståtte. *Gedenke-
  undDokumentationsståtte KZDrütte.* June 2016.

Matrikelamt Der Israelitischen Kultusgemeinde in Wien. "Death Certificate
  Frieda Chinkes." Vienna, September 1948.

McLean, Karen Spence and Marjane Telck. *Coal Camps of Sweetwater County.*
  Charleston: Arcadia Publishing, 2012.

Museum, Washington D.C. Holocaust. 2015. https://www.ushmm.org.

Petrovic, Lidija. Daughter of Eva Timar. Interview by author. August 3,  2016.

Republic of Poland. "Unabridged Copy of Marriage Certificate." Trans. Marek
  Zaluski. Warszawa: Register Office, Republic of Poland, January 24, 1909.

Saidel, Rochelle G. *The Jewish Women of Ravensbrück Concentration Camp.*
  Madison: The University of Wisconsin Press, 2006.

Stanley, Dean L. and Dwight L. Diller (eds). *Frankfurt am Main.* Frankfurt:
  United States Headquarters Command, circa 1945.

Steinke, Karolin. *Trains to Ravensbrück Transports by the Reichsbahn
  1939-1945.* Berlin: Metropol Verlag, 2009.

Turner, Margot. Interview by author. Garland, Texas, 2015.

Zacharias, Elke. Interview by author. April 2016.

# Acknowledgments

⊰❀⊱

I have many people to thank for all the help they have given me.

Margot Turner, Margit's close childhood and lifelong friend, answered all my questions with patience and provided me with much insight to my mother and her early life.

Ruth Grosch, Margit's half-sister, was very gracious and willing to share her knowledge of how she and my mother were reunited, and Hugo Kühner's autograph book.

Fran Swan gave me much-needed love and encouragement, and contributed her editing ability and her willingness to share her Jewish background with me. I could not have done this without her.

Elke Zacharias, the director/curator of the Watenstedt/Salzgitter Memorial, provided me with much documentation of the concentration camps and expertise in interpreting it. Her willingness to personally take me on the journey of the KZ camps provided me with insight otherwise unattainable.

Werner Will, himself an author, expertly translated documents and my Opa's memoir.

Karen Judy helped me greatly with the family tree and genealogy research.

Rye Svingen and my son, Lucas, developed the maps.

My daughter, Amber Majnik, took a special interest in this book and edited each and every version I wrote.

I could not have written this book without my husband, Tom, who was a tireless cheerleader, my guide in our travels, and gave me writing and editing suggestions throughout the project.

# Appendix A—Documents

TRANSLATION FROM POLISH

National Emblem
THE REPUBLIC OF POLAND
Mazowieckie Province
Register Office in State Capitol Warszawa
Nr. ZB-1007/7/1909 Tarnopol, Date January 24, 1909

## UNABRIDGED COPY OF MARRIAGE CERTIFICATE
### I.   Records regarding persons getting married

|  | Man | Woman |
|---|---|---|
| 1. Last name | Chinkes----------------------------- | Kuj------------------------------------ |
| 2. Given name(s) | Izaak Leib------------------------- | Marjem----------------------------- |
| 3. Family name | Chinkes ------------------------- | Kuj------------------------------------ |
| 4. Marital status | Single----------------------------- | Single--------------------------------- |
| 5. Date of birth | 1872----------------------------- | June 21, 1884---------------------- |
| 6. Place of birth | Mikulince----------------------- | Tarnopol----------------------------- |
| 7. Place of living | Tarnopol------------------------ | Tarnopol----------------------------- |

### II.   Records regarding date and place of the wedding
1. Date: Twenty fourth of January nineteen hundred nine
(24.01.1909) year                          2. Place: Tarnopol

### III.   Records regarding parents
A. Father

| | | |
|---|---|---|
| 1. Last name | ------------------------------------- | ------------------------------------- |
| 2. Given name(s) | ------------------------------------- | Izaak Mendel--------------------- |
| 3. Family name | ------------------------------------- | Stein---------------------------------- |
| B. Mother. | | |
| 1. Last name | ------------------------------------- | ------------------------------------- |
| 6.Given name | Sima Roza----------------------- | Henna--------------------------------- |
| 7. Family name | Chinkes-------------------------- | Kuj------------------------------------ |

### IV.   Last name used after wedding
1. Man: Chinkes ----------------------------------------------------------------
2. Woman: Chinkes ---------------------------------------------------------------
3. Children: Chinkes ----------------------------------------------------------------

*Marriage certificate of Izaak Chinkes and Marjem Kuj (page 1)*

## IV. Nazwisko noszone po zawarciu małżeństwa:

1. Mężczyzny   **Chinkes**-----------------------------------------

2. Kobiety   **Chinkes**-----------------------------------------

3. Dzieci   **Chinkes**-----------------------------------------

## V. Świadkowie:

| 1. Nazwisko . . . . | **Babad**------------ | **Ludwak**----------- |
|---|---|---|
| 2. Imię . . . . . . | **Józef**------------ | **Chaskel**---------- |

## VI. Uwagi: Akt sporządzono w dniu 24 stycznia 1909-----

**roku w Izraelickim Urzędzie Metrykalnym w**------------

**Tarnopolu.**------------------------------------------

--------------------------------------------------------

Podpisy osób zawierających małżeństwo i świadków:

| /-/ Chinkes Izaak | /-/ Babad Józef |
|---|---|
| /-/ Kuj Marjem | /-/ Ludwak Chaskel |

Stwierdzam, że osoby wymienione w rubryce I złożyły
zgodne oświadczenia o wstąpieniu w związek małżeński.

**KIEROWNIK**
**/-/ Rabin Szymon Babad**
Urzędu Stanu Cywilnego

**Wzmianki dodatkowe:** _____

--------------------------------------------------------

Poświadcza się zgodność powyższego odpisu z treścią aktu w księdze małżeństw.

| Miejsce na opłatę skarbową | ......................**Warszawa**......, data **11.05.2006** |
|---|---|

**INSPEKTOR**
**KIEROWNIK** ttry
Urzędu Stanu Cywilnego
mgr Teresa Tryfon

m.p.

M-5 PTH „Technika", Gliwice

*Marriage certificate of Izaak Chinkes and Marjem Kuj (page 2)*
Source: Consulate General of the Republic of Poland, Los Angeles, CA

*Margit Chinkes birth certificate*
*Source: Personal files of Margit Chinkes Pascetti*

# Totenschein.

VON dem Unterzeichneten wird bestätigt, daß laut hieramtlichen Sterbebuches

Jahrgang ___1931___ Reihezahl ___1967___

Frieda C h i n k e s

geb.am 27.II.1910 in Tarnopol,zust.n.Tarnopol

Gewesene Wohnung:Wien,II.Franz Hochedlingerg.3

Sterbeort:II.Donaukanal bei Augartenbrücke

Todesursache: Tod durch Ertrinken

am ___7.VI.1931 siebenten Juni___

im Jahre Eintausend ___neun___ hundert ___einunddreissig___ starb

und am ___11___ ten ___Juni___ 19 31

auf dem katholischen xisraelischen Friedhofe in Wien beerdigt wurde.

Wien, am ___14.September___ 19 48

MATRIKELAMT DER
ISRAELITISCHEN KULTUSGEMEINDE
IN WIEN

*Frieda Chinkes death certificate*
*Source: Personal files of Margit Chinkes Pascetti*

*Oma's German ID card*
Source: Margit Chinkes Pascetti personal files

8-1-44

Den 1. 8. 44.

Liebe Oma!

Soeben habe ich erkennen müssen, daß alles aus ist. Ein paar Jahre muß ich in ein Lager. Bei mir war eine Jugendführerin. Oma ich kann kaum schreiben. Dieses ist nun das ungütige Ende. Hätte ich hier die Hanni so wäre sie Brei. Nur sie ist an allem Unglück schuld. Ich kann die Tränen kaum zurückhalten, trotzdem sie nichts mitern. Der ganze Fall ist bei der Geheimen Staatspolizei in der Lindenstr. in der Hand. Gehe noch einmal dahin. Du mußt mit der Straßenbahn Linie 3 fahren. Tue diesen letzten Bittgang. Ich flehe Dich darum. Ich kann nix mehr machen. Auf Wiedersehen Es küßt Dich herzlich und alle Bekannten

Margit.

*Margit's letter to her Oma from the detention center*
*Source: Margit Chinkes Pascetti personal files*

*Margit's letter to her father from the detention center*
*Source: Margit Chinkes Pascetti personal files*

*Margit's concentration camp prisoner record card*
Source: Ravensbrück Concentration Camp archives

*Postcard sent by Margit from Watenstedt, 1945*
Source: Margit Chinkes Pascetti personal files

*Margit's Certificate of Naturalization 1953*
Source: Margit Chinkes Pascetti personal files

*Transport register of people arriving to Ravensbrück*
Source: Ravensbrück Concentration Camp archives

# Appendix B—Photographs

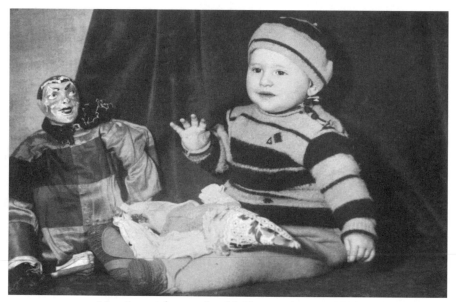

*Margit at eight months old, Vienna, Austria, 1930*
*(Flanzgraben family had this same picture.)*
Source: Margit Chinkes Pascetti personal files

*Hedwig, Hugo's sister, Erfurt, Germany*
Source: Margit Chinkes Pascetti personal files

*Margit with Oma and Hugo, 1936*
Source: Margit Chinkes Pascetti personal files

*Margit and Angelo, Frankfurt am Main, Germany, 1948*
Source: Margit Chinkes Pascetti personal files

Frankfurt a/Main 9.4.49.

My sweetest sweetheart;
To-night I'm really late with
my letter, but I dont know if I have
time, to write to-morrow. How are you?
I hope not sick. You have good weather
on the ship? Here is it awful, always
storm and (real) raining. We are really
lucky if the sun shines for an minit.
I wrote just before I begin this letter, all
the stoff, we have in the big box, of
a paper. It was sure much work. To-
morrow I will make the other box. I
dont know the adresse of your sis sister
Liz, so I send all the letters to your right
sister. Last night, when my father came
home, he brought 2 bottle bottle Likör.
Really test good. But I would give everything away if I could come to you.
I still have louter homesick to you. For
sure, I would go cresy if something
would happen to you. The baby is O.K.
Maybe I take a walk with her to-morrow.
This is everything for today. Dont be mad
but I'm very very tired. Sleep very well
my darling. Good night.
                    Love Margit.

*Love letter to Angelo, April 1949*
*Source: Margit Chinkes Pascetti personal files*

*Ship tickets to USA, June 1949*

*Margit and Angelica on ship*
Source: *Margit Chinkes Pascetti personal files*

*Angelo's sister, Carmen, meeting Margit in Albuquerque, New Mexico, 1949*
*Source: Margit Chinkes Pascetti personal files*

# Autogramme der Großen

## Trauerfeier für Friedenskämpfer Max Hugo Kühner

Max Hugo Kühner ist tot. Der reiselustige Wirt des „Blauen Bock" in der Eschersheimer Landstraße und „Weltenbummler in Sachen Frieden" starb nach langer Krankheit Anfang Mai. Seine Wohnung in Frankfurt hat mittlerweile ihr unverwechselbares Gesicht verloren: Seine Tochter Margit Pascetti war aus Leadville / Colorado angereist, um den Nachlaß zu sichten, zu ordnen, in Kartons zu verpacken, in die Staaten zu schicken, um dort ein Erinnerungs-Archiv aufzubauen — Stück für Stück ging mit Bildern und Urkunden nach der Person auch die „Persönlichkeit" dieser Räume dahin.

Dreierlei hat ihn in Frankfurt und im Rest der Welt „berühmt" und für manche unvergessen gemacht: Er war ein beliebter Frankfurter Gastwirt, er war lange Jahre, auch noch im Rentenalter, im Kultur- und Geselligkeitsverein Nordweststadt engagiert, und er war der „berühmteste Autogrammjäger der Welt".

Schon vor dem Kriege nannte sich Kühner, 1907 in Dresden geboren, „Schriftensammler" — und was er sammelte, waren Autographen, Grußadressen, Worte der Erinnerung von Größen (und solchen, die sich dafür halten) aus Politik und Showgeschäft; er nahm ihm dann die Gestapo ab. Das Ergebnis dieser nach dem Kriege wieder aufgenommenen Sammel-Leidenschaft: Das „Größte Buch der Welt", ein 84 Kilo schwerer Foliant, in dem nicht gerade Gott, aber viel aus der Welt vorkommt.

Darin stehen mit der Verpflichtung für die Friedensidee zum Beispiel die Grußworte der Hochkommissare McCloy („Ich fühle mich geehrt..") und François Poncet. Kühner postulierte damals: „Regierungen kommen und gehen, aber mein Werk wird bleiben. Wenn einer unterschrieben hat und erklärt den Krieg, dann liegt das Buch als Dokument da, und er kann zur Rechenschaft gezogen werden."

Auch ein zweites „Adressen-Buch" spiegelt dies und das der Zeitgeschichte: Nach etwa Konrad Adenauer und Theodor Heuss als Gründungs-Größen der Bundesrepublik im „Größten Buch der Welt" finden sich im zweiten, kleineren Folianten ermunternde Worte von Hessen-Figuren wie zum Beispiel Albert Osswald, ehemals Ministerpräsident, oder Lia Wöhr oder Heinz Schenk, für hessischen Humor zuständig — schon eine kuriose Mischung.

Die früheren Gäste der „Vier Jahreszeiten" in Zeilsheim, später des „Südstern" in Sachsenhausen und des „Blauen Bock" werden sich nicht nur an den Weltenbummler und Einzelkämpfer für den Frieden, von dem auch amerikanische, englische, französische Zeitungs-Archive künden, erinnern, sie werden ebenso wie die Vereinsmitglieder in der Nordweststadt eines „Frankfurters aus Sachsen", des ersten Fastnachtsprinzen nach dem Kriege übrigens, gedenken. — Heute um 11.30 findet auf dem Hauptfriedhof die Trauerfeier statt. per

Unterwegs mit dem „Größten Buch der Welt": Max Hugo Kühner in den 50er Jahr

*Newspaper obituary article about Hugo and his*
*130-pound autograph book, May 1990*

*Ruth with husband and daughter, Angelika, 1952*
Source: Margit Chinkes Pascetti personal files

*Last Pascetti family picture, November 1995;*
*left to right: Angelo, Gerald, Margit, Roxana, Angelica*
*Source: Angelica Osborne personal files*

*Ruth and Margit, 1993*
Source: *Margit Chinkes Pascetti personal files*

*The author, Angie Osborne, Ruth Grosch,*
*and Tom Osborne in Bad Tennstedt, Germany, April 2016*
Source: *Angelica Osborne personal files*

# Appendix C
## The Story of German
## SS-Captain Theodor Johann Brueing

⟨◈⟩

Camp commandant of Salzgitter-Watenstedt subcamp was SS-Captain Theodor Johann Breuing, born on Nov 14, 1890 at Recklinghausen/Northrhine-Westfalia. He had completed training as a teacher in 1912, had served in World War I at last as officer, had been taken prisoner-of-war and was released in October 1919.

Breuing was a determined Catholic and joined the Catholic Centre Party. In 1936 he joined the staff of the Paulusschule of Recklinghausen. Soon after the Nazi party came to power he joined organizations affiliated to that party and then the party itself. He held minor political functions as instructor of the local group of the party and local head of its welfare branch. He was foreman of his school for air raid protection and for cinematic political propaganda. In World War two he was too old for combat duties and therefore at first employed as part time police officer in his hometown.

In April 1941 he was drafted into the German army and posted to a prisoner-of-war camp near Kaunas in the Soviet Union. In May 1944 he was transferred to the armed SS and sent to Neuengamme for guard duties. He hadn't volunteered for this. To transfer thousands of elderly soldiers to concentration camps was due to organizational changes in the exploitation of the slave labour of the prisoners.

The German ministry of armament and war production had criticized that it was not efficient enough to put up factories on the camp sites. Improvement would make it necessary to take the prisoners to the production sites of the German industry. That was the take-off of the system of subcamps. Neuengamme main camp controlled at last 87 subcamps scattered throughout the northern half of Germany. The crucial point of this policy change for the SS was that it was under-staffed for carrying out the largely extended guard duties. As the prisoners were employed on behalf of the regular military, Himmler had demanded that the army should help and Hitler had consented.

Breuing was one of 1,500 army and soldiers and 1,000 seamen of the German navy to join the Neuengamme guard battalion. The armed SS appointed Breuing to "SS-Hauptsturmführer" which was an equivalent to his army rank and used him from the beginning on for tasks with leadership responsibility. Senior prisoners

*Captain Theodor Johann Brueing*

of the three subcamps of Salzgitter have testified in postwar trials that Breuing was in favour of the prisoners and therefore had conflicts with his hard boiled SS-NCOs.

In the last weeks of the war he had to organize and to supervise the evacuation of the prisoners. A large group of whom was boarded on a train destined to Bergen Belsen camp. Breuing went there by car but couldn't meet this transport as it had been redirected to Ravensbrück camp for women. As he was not informed of this he had lost his prisoners. For a week he hastened around in vain to find them. He knew that he would be humiliated by the camp commandant and therefore hesitated to return to the camp.

In a rural inn two miles away from Neuengamme camp he met two other SS-officers and drank alcohol with them. Having been notified, the adjutant of the camp went to that pub and arrested all three. In contrast to his two fellows Breuing was completely drunk.

The camp commandant ordered all three to stand trial before the Hamburg court martial of the SS. On April 24, 1945 Breuing was sentenced to death and the two others were acquitted. Two days later Breuing was shot on the rifle range of the camp. The camp commandant had ordered the whole guard battalion to be present. In his address he threatened everybody neglecting his duties in Germany's most difficult hour would share the fate of the doomed man.

The sources of my biographical sketch are unpublished records. Attached you find a copy of the death notification newspaper add (sic)of Breuing's family which leaves the true status of the deceased as SS-officer undisclosed.

The photograph showing Breuing is taken from the book: *Chronik der Paulusschule: Die Zeit der Volksschule 1908-1968*. Eine Festgabe zum 90jährigen Bestehen der Paulusschule Recklinghausen. Ed. Luitgard Nolte. Recklinghausen: Rudolf Winkelmann publishers 1997.

Yours sincerely,
Mit freundlichen Grüßen
Dr. Reimer Möller
KZ-Gedenkstätte Neuengamme

(reprinted with the permission of Dr. Reimer Möller)